1965

MILITARY TRANSPORTS AND TRAINING AIRCRAFT OF THE WORLD

MILITARY TRANSPORTS AND TRAINING AIRCRAFT OF THE WORLD

F. G. SWANBOROUGH

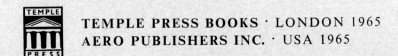

TEMPLE PRESS BOOKS · LONDON 1965
AERO PUBLISHERS INC. · USA 1965

First Published 1965

© 1965 FREDERICK GORDON SWANBOROUGH

Library of Congress Catalog Card Number
65–26307

Published in the United States by
AERO PUBLISHERS, INC.

Printed in Great Britain by
Morrison & Gibb Ltd., London and Edinburgh

CONTENTS

INTRODUCTION

IN 'COMBAT AIRCRAFT OF THE WORLD', a companion volume to this work, the offensive aircraft of the major World powers have been described. The operational deployment of fighters and bombers—should the occasion arise—depends, however, on a wide range of second-line aircraft which are needed to maintain flight crew efficiency and to establish lines of supply.

These are the aircraft with which the present volume is concerned—the trainers on which aircrews obtain their primary instruction and continuation training; the transports which give tactical support to the front-line units in the field and operate strategic air-supply routes around the World; and the variety of miscellaneous smaller types operated by Air Forces, Armies and Navies for communications, liaison and similar duties.

The arrangement of the material is similar to that adopted in the earlier volumes in the series—*Combat Aircraft*, *Turbine-engined Airliners* and *Vertical Flight Aircraft*. While the text describes the origins, development and operational features of the aircraft, the illustrations have been chosen to show each variant from prototype to latest production model, and to depict the service markings of the various users of each type. Once again, full-page plates of the more important types have been included.

Distinguishing between those types to be included in this volume and those to be excluded has been a difficult exercise. All types currently in production or under development at the present time have been included; in addition, as many as possible of the aircraft no longer in production but still significant in their service use have been included. The choice in this final category is necessarily an arbitrary one and is the author's own. Advanced proficiency and conversion trainers derived from single-seat fighters have not been included, since they are fully described in *Combat Aircraft*.

It is pleasant to record the ready assistance extended during the compilation of this volume by numerous companies and individuals. They include the majority of the companies whose products are described herein and the air attaches and public information officers of a large number of Air Forces. Additional photographs were drawn from the files of *The Aeroplane*; the loan of others by William Green and J. W. R. Taylor is gratefully acknowledged.

MAY, 1965.   F. G. SWANBOROUGH

AERO COMMANDER U-4, U-9 (U.S.A.)

VERSIONS OF THE Aero Commander light twin have been in service with both the U.S.A.F. and U.S. Army since 1953. The Commander design itself originated with a prototype which was first flown on April 23, 1948. The first production model, the Aero Commander 520, appeared in 1952 and three examples of this version were procured for evaluation in 1953 under the Army designation YL-26. Three more Aero Commander 520s were supplied to the South Korean Air Force at the instigation of the U.S. authorities.

A single example of the more powerful Aero Commander 560 was evaluated by the U.S.A.F. as the YL-26A and a batch of 15 was then procured with the designation L-26B. These were allocated to M.A.T.S. and to other U.S.A.F. units for use as Staff transports. A single L-26B was also procured by the U.S. Army.

With 320 h.p. Lycoming engines, the Aero Commander 680 Super was the next version purchased by the U.S. services. Two supplied to the U.S.A.F. were assigned to V.V.I.P. duties, including Presidential transportation, as L-26Cs, while four more went to the Army for similar V.V.I.P. duties.

One L-26 was modified for the U.S. Army Signal Corps by the University of Illinois to carry Motorola sideways-looking airborne radar (SLAR) built into the fuselage. After trials with this conversion, two more examples were purchased as RL-26Ds.

When the U.S. Defense Department introduced a unified designating system for aircraft of all three services in 1962, the L-26 was left with two designations in what appeared to be a clerical error which, in this particular case, negated the purpose of the scheme. The aircraft used by the U.S.A.F. had become U-4s during 1961, and those serving with the Army were re-designated U-9s in 1962. In detail the re-designating of the types mentioned above was as follows:

L-26B (U.S.A.F.)	to	U-4A
L-26B (Army)	to	U-9B
L-26C (U.S.A.F.)	to	U-4B
L-26C (Army)	to	U-9C
L-26D (Army)	to	U-9D
RL-26D (Army)	to	RU-9D

The Aero Commander normally provides seating for three to five passengers in addition to two pilots, with full dual control. The military aircraft assigned to V.I.P. duties had three passenger seats in addition to the two pilots.

Span, 49 ft. 6 in.; length, 35 ft. 11¼ in.; height, 14 ft. 6 in.; wing area, 255 sq. ft.; aspect ratio, 9.45.

Empty weight, 4,650 lb.; gross weight, 7,500 lb.

Max. speed, 250 m.p.h. at sea level; cruising speed, 205 m.p.h. at 10,000 ft.; initial rate of climb, 1,587 ft./min.; service ceiling, 21,900 ft.; take-off distance to 50 ft., 1,350 ft.; landing distance from 50 ft., 1,375 ft.; range, 1,150 miles with normal load.

1. *Aero Commander U-4B, U.S.A.F.*
2. *Aero Commander RU-9D, U.S. Army.*
3. *Aero Commander U-9C, U.S. Army.*

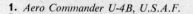

ANTONOV An-2 (U.S.S.R.)

An Antonov An-2 in Hungarian civil markings.

ONE OF THE MOST WIDELY PRODUCED Soviet aeroplanes of post-War design, the An-2 was the first product of the design bureau headed by Oleg K. Antonov. The prototype made its first flight in 1947 and appears to have been designed as a general purpose or utility aeroplane with particular attention to agricultural duties. Its original designation of SKh-1, derived from a Russian title meaning "agricultural economic", emphasized this rôle.

Subsequently, the An-2, as it soon became known, found many other applications, both military and civil. Its outstanding features were the capacious fuselage, rugged structure, ease of maintenance and good field performance. The biplane layout, which might appear as an anachronism in a post-War aeroplane, was justified by the low-speed performance and short take-off and landing distances which were made possible by the large wing area. Both upper and lower wings have electrically-actuated slotted flaps and slotted ailerons and auto slots at the leading edge are used on the upper wing alone.

The An-2 is provided with a large freight door in the port side of the fuselage, a smaller passenger door being incorporated within it. The cabin can accommodate up to 14 paratroops; 7–10 passengers in airline-type seats; six stretchers and attendant or 2,750 lb. of freight. The cockpit, with accommodation for two pilots (with dual controls) and a flight engineer, is forward of and above the cabin.

Initial production versions were powered by 630 h.p. ASh-21 engines, but the 1,000 h.p. ASh-621R was later standardized, driving a four-blade constant speed propeller with curved or scimitar-shaped blades.

The An-2 was ordered in large quantities for use by the Soviet Air Force as a utility transport, paratroop trainer and ambulance. It has been supplied for military and civil use in virtually all the nations associated with the U.S.S.R.—notably those of the East European bloc and China.

A production line for An-2s was established in China at the State Aircraft Factory at Shen Yang, near Mukden. The first An-2 from this factory flew in late 1957 or early 1958 and the type was believed to be still in production there in 1964. A little later, the An-2 went into production at the W.S.K. (Transport Equipment Manufacturing Centre) of the Polish state-owned industry at Mielec. This factory supplied An-2s to the Polish Air Force and for civil use in Poland, and also became the prime source of spares support for the type after it had gone out of production in Russia.

The An-2 can be operated on skis or on floats in place of the usual wheeled undercarriage. The floatplane version is sometimes referred to as the An-2V (or by its design bureau number, An-6) but this may refer only to the civil variant. Apart from having 24 ft. 6 in. floats the An-2V differs from the standard aircraft in having a straight-bladed propeller.

To permit the installation of pumping and spraying equipment beneath the fuselage for insecticide, the An-2S agricultural version has a long-stroke landing gear. Lighter than the An-2, the An-2S operates in civil guise.

An interesting version of the aircraft developed for high altitude meteorological research was designated An-2ZA. This aircraft, operated in military markings by a Soviet research establishment, had a turbo-supercharger on its ASh-621R/TK engine, which maintained an output of 850 h.p. up to 31,000 ft. An observation station was built into the base of the fin so that the build-up of ice on the airframe could be watched. This particular aircraft set a World class record with a climb to 36,903 ft. in June 1954.

The An-2 has the NATO code-name *Colt.*

Span, upper wing, 59 ft. 7½ in.; span, lower wing, 46 ft. 8½ in.; length, 42 ft. 0 in.; height, 13 ft. 7½ in.; wing area, 770 sq. ft.; sweepback, nil.
Empty weight, 7,275 lb.; payload, 2,735 lb.; gross weight, 11,575 lb.
Max. speed, 161 m.p.h. at sea level (floatplane 153 m.p.h.); cruising speed, 124 m.p.h.; service ceiling, 16,400 ft.; take-off run, 300 ft.; landing run, 250 ft.; range, 560 miles with max. payload; 1,085 miles with 1,650 lb. payload.

1. *A Soviet Air Force An-2 dropping parachutists.*
2. *An An-2 at take-off.*
3 *and* **4.** *Antonov An-2s at a Soviet airfield.*

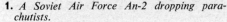

ANTONOV An-4, An-12 (U.S.S.R.)

An Antonov An-12 in service with the Iraqi Air Force.

AFTER COMPLETING WORK on the An-2, the Antonov design bureau in Kiev turned its attention to a Soviet Air Force requirement for a twin-engined tactical transport—a class of aircraft which had previously received little serious attention in the U.S.S.R. Only one earlier Soviet-designed transport, in fact, had achieved quantity production—the Il-12/Il-14 family. Appearing in public for the first time in June 1956, the new Antonov transport was intended to replace the Il-12/Il-14 but its service use was restricted by poor performance. It was designated An-4 in service with the Soviet Air Force (and An-8 by the design bureau). A few were still in service in 1964, and were identified by the NATO code name *Camp*.

The An-4, powered by two 5,100 e.h.p. Kuznetsov turboprops and capable of accommodating 40 equipped troops, set the pattern for the subsequent development by the Antonov team of a larger transport for both civil and military use. This was the An-10, first flown in March 1957 and having the same layout as the An-4—i.e. high wing, landing gear in fuselage-side blisters, tall, angular tail with dorsal fin. The An-10 was at first powered by Kuznetsov turboprops but the more efficient Ivchenko AI-20 was chosen for production aircraft.

The An-10 went into production to serve with Aeroflot as a large capacity freighter or "airbus", while a military variant was produced in parallel as a tactical transport. Designated An-12 (NATO identification *Cub*), this military version had a re-modelled rear fuselage with loading ramp which can be lowered in flight for air-drop operations and a tail-gunner's position at the base of the rudder.

The cross-section of the An-10/An-12 fuselage is one of the largest of any freighting aircraft produced to date, with a maximum width of 162 inches and a headroom of 108 inches. This means that the aircraft can carry a large proportion of the vehicles and other Army equipment which would need to be air delivered in a military engagement.

Maximum loads of the military version are not known, but can be estimated from details of the An-10 as used by Aeroflot. This can accommodate 130 passengers in a single-class layout, suggesting that the An-12 as a trooper probably could carry at least 150 paratroops. The commercial payload is 32,000 lb. and the An-12 probably can carry a similar load, the extra weight of the ramp and rear gun position being offset by the saving on airline-type seats and cabin trimmings.

The An-12 has a pressurized fuselage and is powered by four 4,015 e.h.p. Ivchenko AI-20 turboprops. Fuel is carried in the wing, which has double-slotted Fowler type flaps to help provide the aircraft's short-field capability. Operations from unprepared landing strips present little difficulty for the An-12 which has comparatively low-pressure tyres on the bogie main units of the landing gear. Skis have also been designed for, and used by, the Antonov An-10 and An-12, which is probably the largest landplane ever operated on skis.

The An-12 is the standard transport in service with the A-V.D.V. (Aviation of the Airborne Troops) units of the Soviet Air Force. An-12s have also occasionally been seen bearing civil Soviet markings—usually to avoid diplomatic complication when visiting foreign countries.

Sixteen examples of the An-12 were purchased for use by the Indian Air Force as part of its programme to provide modern airlift capability in the Himalayan region. Examples of the An-12 are also known to be in service with the air forces of Indonesia, Iraq and the United Arab Republic. One was supplied to Ghana Airways.

Span, 124 ft. 8 in.; length, 121 ft. 3 in.; height, 32 ft. 1 in.; wing area, 1,292 sq. ft.; sweepback, nil.
Gross weight, 121,500 lb.
Cruising speed, 342 m.p.h. at 25,000 ft.; initial rate of climb, 1,970 ft./min.; take-off run, 2,460 ft.; landing run, 2,300 ft.; range, 1,240 miles with 31,970 lb. payload.

1 *and* 2. *Unarmed Antonov An-12s operating freight services for Aeroflot.*
3. *The An-12 9G-AAZ operated by Ghana Airways.*
4. *An Iraqi Air Force An-12.*

BEAGLE AUSTER (Great Britain)

A Beagle-Auster D.5/160 built by OGMA for the Portuguese Air Force.

VARIANTS OF THE AUSTER air observation post and liaison monoplane have been in production in Britain since 1939, when Taylorcraft Aeroplanes (England) Ltd. set up a factory to build under licence the Taylorcraft lightplane designed in America. The name Auster was adopted for the military versions of the Taylorcraft which were used throughout the War, and the name of the manufacturing company was subsequently changed to Auster Aircraft to identify it with its most famous product.

Nearly 2,000 Austers of the Mks. 1 to 7 were built, all closely related. The next production version, the Auster AOP.9, was a complete redesign. First flown on March 19, 1954, it is powered by a 180 h.p. Blackburn Bombardier 203 engine and is equipped to perform a wide range of military duties.

The Auster 9 has a normal crew of two, pilot and observer. The observer sits behind the pilot in a swivelling seat to face forward or aft as required. An optional third seat can be fitted alongside the pilot.

Access to the cabin, through three wide doors, makes it easy to load supplies, light freight, or a stretcher when the aircraft is being used for casualty evacuation. To simplify rapid change between rôles, the Auster 9 has a detachable rear floor in the cabin, held by six bolts so that it can be simply changed. In addition to light liaison and A.O.P. duties, the Auster 9 can be used for supply and mail dropping, cable laying, aerial photography, "sky shouting" and so on.

Structurally, the Auster 9 resembles earlier aircraft in the series, with a tubular metal fuselage frame and all-metal wing. To obtain the best possible field performance, it is provided with split flaps, which are supplemented by drooping ailerons.

The Auster AOP.9 went into production in 1954 and deliveries began early in 1955. Some of the first aircraft delivered went to No. 656 Squadron of the R.A.F. operating in Malaya. After the Army Air Corps had assumed responsibility for its own light liaison flights, the Auster 9 became its principal equipment, until supplemented by helicopters. Production continued until 1960 and Auster 9s were

supplied also to the Indian Army and Air Force and the South African Air Force.

As a private venture in 1961, after the Auster Company had become a part of the Beagle concern, a prototype Auster Mk. 11 was produced. This aircraft (XP254 and later G-ASCC) was essentially a Mk. 9 with a 260 h.p. Continental IO-470 engine, a spatted undercarriage and other detail improvements. It first flew on August 18, 1961.

Various of the civil Auster lightplanes have been purchased from time to time for military duties in only slightly modified form. These include two Autocars supplied to the Royal Australian Navy; a number of Autocrats supplied to the Royal Arab Air Force and Aiglet Trainers used by the Pakistan Air Force. In 1961, the Portuguese Government acquired a licence to build the Auster D.4 and D.5 lightplanes for military training and communications duties. Approximately 100 had been built by 1964.

The Auster D.4 and D.5 are the latest versions of the Auster Autocrat/Aiglet family, from which they differ primarily in having Lycoming engines. These aircraft are thus directly descended from the original Taylorcraft D which wa supplied to the R.A.F. in 1939 for evaluation.

Data for the Auster AOP.9:
Span, 36 ft, 5 in.; length, 23 ft. 8½ in.; height, 8 ft. 11 in.; wing area, 198 sq. ft.
Empty weight, 1,590 lb.; gross weight, 2,125 lb. (2,330 lb. overload case).
Max. speed, 127 m.p.h.; cruising speed, 110 m.p.h.; initial rate of climb, 920 ft./min.; absolute ceiling, 18,500 ft.; take-of distance to 50 ft., 675 ft.; landing distance from 50 ft., 600 ft.

1

2

3

4

1. *A British Army Auster AOP.6 with combination wheel/skid gear.*
2. *An Auster AOP.9 with underwing tank.*
3. *Indian Air Force Auster AOP.9.*
4. *The Beagle Auster AOP.11 prototype.*

BEAGLE **B.206R BASSET** (Great Britain)

The Beagle 206-Z2 Basset prototype in military markings.

ORDERED IN MAY 1963 as the first new communications aircraft purchased by the Royal Air Force in more than a decade, the Beagle B.206R is also the first original product of Beagle Aircraft Ltd. The design had its origin in a project of Bristol Aircraft Ltd. before the latter became part of the British Aircraft Corporation. The design rights in this project, the Bristol 220, were obtained by Mr. Peter Masefield when he left Bristol to become managing director of Beagle during 1960.

The Beagle company was established in the autumn of 1960 and work began at once on construction of a prototype of a development of the Bristol 220 project called the Beagle 206. This first prototype was identified as the B.206X, registered G-ARRM and first flown on August 15, 1961. It was a low-wing five-seat all-metal monoplane powered by two 260 h.p. Continental IO-470 engines, with a span of 38 ft. and gross weight of 6,300 lb.

To fulfil the military requirement for an Anson replacement a seven-seater was needed and the B.206 was consequently developed to have this better load-carrying ability. Within the same overall length, the fuselage was modified to introduce a third seat row to make the aircraft a basic seven- or occasional eight-seater. An increase in wing span to 43 ft. improved the climb performance and the gross weight increased to 7,125 lb. The engines were changed to 310 h.p. Continental GIO-470s.

A prototype was built to the new standard, called the B.206Y (G-ARXM) and first flown on August 12, 1962. In the course of the 13-month period of flight testing for certification which followed, further increases were made in the wing span, first to 45 ft. with the tips at a dihedral angle of 5 degrees and then to 45 ft. 9 in. with the tips at 2 degrees. This defined the production standard.

Also during this period, the Beagle 206 demonstrated its performance in several long distance flights—for example 1,130 miles with a 1,100 lb. payload in 5 hr. 44 min. at 200 m.p.h. The ability to carry a five-man V-bomber crew, plus crew chief and ferry pilot, on missions such as this, was a primary requirement for the Anson-replacement. The excellent single-engined climb of the Beagle 206 was another decisive factor in its favour, and in May 1963 the first military order, for 20 aircraft, was placed. Two pre-production examples had already been ordered by the Ministry of Aviation and these were identified as the B.206Z1 and B.206Z2.

The B.206Z1 (XS742) flew for the first time on January 24, 1964, the third and last of the series to be completed at Shoreham Airport. The B.206Z2 (XS743) followed on February 20, 1964, from Rearsby. Production aircraft for the R.A.F. are designated B.206R Basset while the civil version is the B.206C. A major difference between the two production versions lies in the standard of radio and electronics carried: the B.206R is especially comprehensively equipped, with a Sperry SP-3 auto-pilot, Decca Mk. 8 Flight Log, Rebecca and UHF, VHF, VOR, ILS, ADF and IFF. All this equipment puts up the gross weight of the military version to 7,300 lb. initially and an eventual figure of 7,500 lb. The first production Basset cc. Mk.1 flew on December 27, 1964.

Span, 45 ft. 9 in.; length, 33 ft. 9 in.; height, 11 ft. 3 in.; wing area, 214 sq. ft.; aspect ratio, 10; sweepback, nil.
Empty equipped weight, 4,365 lb.; gross weight, 7,300 lb.
Max. speed, 225 m.p.h. at sea level; cruising speed, 210 m.p.h. at 10,000 ft.; initial rate of climb, 1,500 ft./min.; service ceiling, 20,400 ft.; take-off distance to 50 ft., 1,460 ft.; landing distance from 50 ft., 1,600 ft.; range with capacity payload, 990 miles; range with max. fuel and 1,280 lb. payload, 1,890 miles.

1. *The original Beagle 206-X, G-ARRM.*
2. *The Beagle 206-Y, G-ARXM.*
3. *XS742, the Beagle 206-Z1.*
4. *The Beagle 206-Z2, XS743, on the ground.*

BEECH U-8 SEMINOLE (U.S.A.)

Beechcraft U-8F twin engined command transport, U.S. Army.

PRIMARY COMMUNICATIONS aircraft in service with the U.S. Army since 1953, the U-8 Seminole is the military equivalent of the Twin Bonanza light twin. Until 1962, these aircraft were designated L-23 in the liaison category, the first four having been purchased in 1951 and evaluated at Fort Sill, Oklahoma as YL-23s in 1952.

These were standard six-seat Twin Bonanzas, purchased by the Army "off-the-shelf", and at 6,000 lb. they were the heaviest twin-engined aircraft operated by the Army at the time of delivery. Successful evaluation led to production orders being placed in 1952 for 55 L-23As, and these went into service with U.S. Army units at home and overseas. They were supplemented by 40 L-23Bs, which differed primarily in having metal in place of wooden propellers.

The U.S.A.F. evaluated a single example of the Twin Bonanza with the designation XL-23C. Subsequent models in the series, designated up to L-23F, were re-designated in the U-8 category, and include the following types:

U-8D. Improvements in the commercial model of the Twin Bonanza were also adopted by the U.S. Army. The commercial E50 model of 1954 introduced 340 h.p. supercharged O-480 engines and these were adopted, together with other detail refinements. The Army ordered 85 of this version, with deliveries starting in November 1956.

In addition to production of new U-8Ds, all surviving L-23As and L-23Bs (a total of 93) went through a re-manufacturing programme to bring them up to U-8D (L-23D) standard. These aircraft were treated as new in most respects, including the allocation of new serial numbers.

U-8E. Six examples of the commercial D50 model of the Twin Bonanza were purchased off-the-shelf by the Army in 1956. These had two 295 h.p. Lycoming GO-480-G2D6 engines.

RU-8D. Eight aircraft with this designation were used by the U.S. Army in its programme to develop SLAR (sideways-looking airborne radar) as an aid for battlefield surveillance. The equipment requires a long slender container, which was carried under the fuselage of the RU-8D. Two types of SLAR were used in these trials—Motorola APS-85 and Texas Instruments APQ-86.

U-8F. Using the wings and tail unit of the Twin Bonanza, the Beech Queen Air was introduced in 1958 as an all-weather executive aircraft. The major external difference between the two types was the deepening of the rear fuselage to increase the cabin capacity.

Three examples of the Queen Air, with 340 h.p. Lycoming engines, were delivered to the Army establishment at Fort Rucker in March 1959 for a full evaluation. This was successful and a production order was placed for an initial batch of 18. Other contracts have followed. Like the earlier models, the U-8F seats six. Its performance is superior to that of the earlier versions.

A later version of the Queen Air, the 65-80 with 380 h.p. engines and a swept-back fin and rudder, has been ordered by the Japanese Maritime Self-Defence Force.

NU-8F. Early in 1963, Beech converted a Queen Air 65-80 to have two Pratt & Whitney PT-6 turboprop engines. Apart from the engine change and addition of a ventral fin, this aircraft was similar to the Army's U-8Es. It served as the prototype for the similarly-engined Beech King Air before being assigned to the U.S. Army for evaluation in 1964. For these trials it was given the designation NU-8F.

Data for the U-8F:
Span, 45 ft. 10½ in.; length, 33 ft. 4 in.; height, 14 ft. 2 in.; wing area, 277 sq. ft.; aspect ratio, 7.51.
Empty weight, 4,996 lb.; gross weight, 7,700 lb.
Max. speed, 240 m.p.h.; cruising speed, 200 m.p.h.; initial rate of climb, 1,300 ft./min.; service ceiling, 31,300 ft.; take-off distance to 50 ft., 1,560 ft.; landing distance from 50 ft., 1,685 ft.; range, 1,200 miles with appropriate reserves.

---

1. *Beechcraft L-23A, U.S. Army.*
2. *Beechcraft RU-8D with Motorola APS-85 SLAR.*
3. *Beechcraft RU-8D with AN/UPD-1 SLAR.*
4. *Beechcraft NU-8F with PT-6 turboprops.*

1

2

3

4

BOEING C-135, KC-135 STRATOTANKER (U.S.A.)

Boeing KC-135A tanker-transport.

MORE EXAMPLES of the KC-135 family have been built than any other type of military jet transport or support aircraft. Production ended early in 1965 with 732 of the basic tanker-transports built, plus nearly a hundred other versions.

The need for a high-performance tanker, capable of refuelling Strategic Air Command's B-47 and B-52 bombers, was recognized by the Boeing company before it had been clearly defined by the U.S.A.F. itself. This military requirement played a major part in shaping the private venture Boeing jet transport, the Type 367-80, which became the progenitor not only of the military series but also of the Model 707 and 720 family of commercial jet transports.

The prototype, which has become known as the "Dash Eighty" (from its engineering design number) first flew on July 15, 1954. Less than a month later, the U.S.A.F. announced that it would procure a version of the design as a military tanker and the first contract was signed on October 5, 1954. Details of this initial production version and of subsequent variants are given below.

KC-135A Stratotanker. The KC-135A was purchased by the U.S.A.F. as its first flight-refuelling tanker developed as such and not as a modification of an existing type. Its primary rôle was to support the bombers of Strategic Air Command, part of the deterrent force.

The fuselage of the KC-135A includes an upper deck which can be used to carry 80 passengers or 25 tons of cargo; all flight refuelling equipment is below the main floor. A telescopic "flying boom" is incorporated at the rear end of the fuselage; this boom is controlled by the boom operator, lying prone in the fuselage, who "flies" the boom into the receptacle of the receiving bomber, flying in close formation behind the KC-135A. Fuel is carried in integral wing tanks, in the centre section and in tanks beneath the main cargo floor. The entire 31,200 U.S. gallon capacity is usable by the KC-135A or can be transferred to a receiving aircraft. Power is from four 13,700 lb.s.t. Pratt & Whitney J57-P-59W turbojets.

The first KC-135A was rolled-out at the Boeing Renton plant on July 18, 1956, immediately following the 888th and last KC-97

tanker. It first flew on August 31, 1956 and the U.S.A.F. accepted its first KC-135A on January 31, 1957. Operational service with the new type began on June 18, 1957 with the 93rd Air Refuelling Squadron. Many notable long-distance flights have since been made by KC-135As.

The 732nd and last KC-135A was delivered to the U.S.A.F. on January 12, 1965.

To permit KC-135As to refuel Tactical Air Command aircraft, which use the British-developed probe and drogue refuelling method, equipment has been developed to allow the flying boom to trail the refuelling drogue. Other KC-153s have been adapted for special research tasks and five were modified in 1961 as airborne command posts for S.A.C. The latter have been superceded by EC-135Cs.

C-135A Stratolifter. In February 1961, the U.S.A.F. purchased a number of transport versions of the basic KC-135A, to serve as interim modernization equipment for the Military Air Transport Service which at that time had no jet transports. In the C-135, the refuelling equipment was deleted, and the payload increased to 89,000 lb. or 126 troops. Engines were the same as those in the KC-135A. First of 15 C-135As flew on May 19, 1961 and was delivered to the U.S.A.F. a month later.

C-135B. M.A.T.S. acquired a further 30 of the Boeing transports powered by 18,000 lb. Pratt & Whitney TF33-P-5 turbofan engines. These engines improved the payload-range performance and other characteristics. The first C-135B flew on February 15, 1962 and was delivered to M.A.T.S. 12 days later.

EC-135C. The success of the airborne command post concept, using modified KC-135As, led the U.S.A.F. to order 17 EC-135Cs specially equipped for this duty. The A.C.P. concept, operated by S.A.C., provides that at least one of these aircraft is airborne at all times, carrying control teams who could assume
[Continued on p. 14

1. *Boeing EC-135C airborne command post.*
2. *Boeing C-135A with J57 turbojets.*
3. *Boeing C-135B with TF33 turbofans.*

1

2

3

command of strategic forces in the event that the headquarters command post at Omaha and its alternative were destroyed.

The EC-135C retains full tanker capability and is also equipped to receive fuel from another KC-135. In an emergency, it could withdraw fuel from a bomber through its flying boom. An extensive range of communication equipment is carried. Engines are 18,000 lb.s.t. TF33 turbofans.

The first EC-135C was delivered in July 1964 to S.A.C. at Offutt A.F.B., Nebraska. Four others followed it at Offutt and four each were assigned to H.Q. 8th A.F. (Westover A.F.B., Mass.); H.Q. 2nd A.F. (Barksdale A.F.B.) and H.Q. 15th A.F. (March A.F.B.).

KC-135F. Twelve examples of the tanker were procured by the French Air Force with this designation. The aircraft are assigned as tankers for the Mirage IV *force de frappe*, and are adapted for probe and drogue refuelling. Delivery began in 1964.

4. *Boeing VC-137A in original finish.*
5. *Boeing VC-137A in revised finish.*
6. *Boeing VC-137C "Air Force One".*

RC-135A. Four aircraft with this designation were produced in 1964 for use by M.A.T.S. Air Photographic and Charting Service. They are specially equipped with cameras for the air survey rôle.

RC-135B. Ten specially-equipped versions of the KC-135 were delivered for electronics reconnaissance duties. They carry additional radio and radar, as indicated by a variety of external aerials and radomes, and specialist crew members.

VC-137A. Related to the KC-135 family through common ancestorship in the Dash Eighty, the C-137s are variants of the slightly larger commercial Boeing 707. In May 1958, the U.S.A.F. ordered three examples of the Boeing 707-120 "off-the-shelf" for use by the Special Air Missions Squadron of M.A.T.S. based at Andrews A.F.B., Washington. The aircraft were primarily intended to be used as V.I.P. transports, including Presidential duties; they were equipped with extensive communications equipment and an "airborne headquarters" as well as a 28-seat cabin. Pratt & Whitney J57 engines provided the power.

The first VC-137A flew on April 4, 1959 and entered service a month later.

VC-137B. The three VC-137As were re-engined in 1963 with Pratt & Whitney TF33 turbofans, making them equivalent to the commercial Model 707-120B.

VC-137C. "Air Force One" or the "Flying White House" was ordered late in 1961 as a Presidential Transport. It is equivalent to the commercial Model 707-320B, powered by TF33 turbofans. It went into service on October 21, 1962.

Data for KC-135A:
Span, 130 ft. 10 in.; length, 136 ft. 3 in.; height, 38 ft. 4 in.; wing area, 2,433 sq. ft.
Empty weight, 98,466 lb.; max. gross weight, 297,000 lb.
Max. speed, 585 m.p.h. at 30,000 ft.; cruising speed, 530 m.p.h.; initial rate of climb, 2,000 ft./min.; service ceiling, 50,000 ft.; range, 1,150 st. miles with 120,000 lb. of transfer fuel; 9,200 st. miles using max. fuel.

BRISTOL **BRITANNIA** (Great Britain)

TWENTY-THREE BRITANNIAS have provided a major portion of the airlift capability of R.A.F. Transport Command since their delivery in 1960. They are operated by Nos. 99 and 511 Squadrons, based at Lyneham.

Initial R.A.F. orders for the Britannia were placed in November 1955, with a contract for six of a variant known as the Britannia 253. Subsequent orders brought the total of this variant on order to 20. In addition, in February 1955, the Ministry of Supply had ordered three Britannia 252s which, it was proposed, would be used for long-range trooping by civil airline contractors. These aircraft were eventually delivered to the R.A.F. also, as Britannia C.Mk.2s; the other 20 were designated Britannia C.Mk.1. In detail, the types differed in a number of respects.

Both marks of military Britannia have a freight loading door in the forward fuselage, with provision for the carriage of heavy military equipment. The Britannia C.Mk.2, however, is essentially a mixed-traffic version, and a strengthened floor for freight carrying is provided only in the forward part of the cabin. In the C.Mk.1, an all-metal full-length "floating floor" is used, permitting military equipment to be stowed the full length of the cabin. The midships galley and forward toilets were removed from the Britannia C.Mk.1 to give an uninterrupted cabin space, whereas they are retained in the C.Mk.2 which in most respects is identical with airline versions of the Britannia. As a result of these changes, the Britannia C.Mk.1 can carry 115 troops compared with 99 in the C.Mk.2.

As an ambulance, the Britannia C.Mk.1 can carry 53 stretcher cases plus attendants; the C.Mk.2 can carry only 22 stretchers, plus 39 seated casualties. The 4,445 e.h.p. Bristol Siddeley Proteus 765 turboprop powers the Britannia C.Mk.2, while its military counterpart, the Proteus 255 with water injection, is used in the C.Mk.2.

The first Britannia C.Mk.2 flew on December 29, 1958 but was not delivered until nearly a year later. The other two C.Mk.2s were available for crew training from the Spring of 1959 and deliveries of the C.Mk.1 began in June of that year. Short Bros. & Harland Ltd. designed the modifications needed for freight carrying and for military operation generally. It also built 15 of the C.Mk.1s and the three C.Mk.2s.

Span, 142 ft. 3½ in.; length, 124 ft. 3 in.; height, 37 ft. 6 in.; wing area, 2,075 sq. ft.; aspect ratio, 9.76.
Empty weight, 90,600 lb.; payload, 37,400 lb.; gross weight, 185,000 lb.; max. landing weight, 137,000 lb.
Cruising speed, 353–405 m.p.h.; take-off distance to 50 ft., 8,000 ft.; landing distance from 50 ft., 6,000 ft.; range, 4,268 miles with 37,400 lb. payload or 5,334 miles with 26,000 lb. payload.

1. *Bristol Britannia C.Mk.1 XL636.*
2. *Britannia C.Mk.1 XL635 landing.*
3. *Britannia C.Mk.1 XL636 in Transport Command markings.*

BREGUET 941 (France)

Breguet 941-01 prototype.

SUBJECT OF an officially-sponsored development programme since 1955, the Breguet 941 is the first practical application of the "deflected slipstream" principal to a transport aircraft. Slipstream deflection, as a means of obtaining STOL performance, began to interest the Breguet company shortly after the end of the Second World War. The principal involves the use of large diameter propellers which bathe virtually the entire wing in their slipstream. Large trailing-edge flaps, when extended, deflect this slipstream vertically downwards to provide a lift component; although this is not sufficient to give a vertical take-off or landing, it does substantially reduce take-off and landing distances.

By 1955, Breguet had evolved their "Integral" idea, the heart of which was the wing and powerplant. Four engines were widely spaced on the wing to drive large diameter propellers and a unique transmission was evolved to link all four propellers so that all would remain under power even if an engine should fail.

In 1955, the first official support for the Integral was forthcoming, in the form of a research contract covering construction of a propeller test bench—actually a wing containing four engines and the transmission system. The latter, evolved by Hispano Suiza, had to be compact enough to fit inside the wing leading edge and flexible enough to cope with changes in wing dihedral angle, under load, of more than 1 degree each side.

The test bench having performed satisfactorily, Breguet next obtained a contract to build a flying test-bed, the Breguet Br. 940. With a gross weight of 16,000 lb., the Br. 940 had a span of 57 ft. 5 in. and was powered by four 400 s.h.p. Turboméca Turmo turboprops driving Ratier-Figeac propellers, two left-handed and two right-handed. The trailing edge of the wing incorporated triple-slotted inboard flaps and double-slotted outboard flaps which also served as ailerons. Apart from the wing design, it was conventional in design and construction. The first flight was made on May 21, 1958 and subsequently test programmes were completed at the official test centres of Bretigny and Istres.

The success of these trials led to a further contract for a prototype of a similar but larger design which could fulfil a French Air Force requirement for a tactical STOL transport. Designated the Br. 941, this aircraft first flew on June 1, 1961 and has since completed many convincing demonstrations of its slow-flying ability.

Powered by four 1,185 s.h.p. Turmo IIID turboprops, the Br. 941 has the same overall layout as the Br. 940. The four propellers each have a diameter of 14 ft. 9 in. Double-slotted flaps are used over the entire trailing edge, divided into four segments each side. A fixed, third slot is provided in combination with the two inner segments of flap, which can be deflected to a maximum angle of 100 degrees (i.e. beyond vertical).

The fuselage of the Br. 941 is designed to carry a variety of military loads and incorporates clam-shell rear-loading doors which in production versions will be suitable for air dropping of paratroops and supplies. The military loads can include up to 16,500 lb. of equipment, 55 paratroops or 24 stretchers.

In 1963, provision was made in the French defence budget for an appropriation to initiate production of the Br. 941 and authorization to produce four examples was given in 1965.

Span, 76 ft. 8 in.; length, 77 ft. 11 in.; height, 30 ft. 8 in.; wing area, 897 sq. ft.; aspect ratio, 6.53; sweepback, nil.
Empty equipped weight, 28,920 lb.; max. take-off weight (assault), 44,000 lb.; (logistic) 52,900 lb.; (long-range) 58,400 lb.; max. landing weight, 41,900 lb. (for 790 ft./min. rate of descent).
Max. cruise speed, 300 m.p.h. at 10,000 ft.; normal cruise, 246 m.p.h. at 10,000 ft.; min. flight speed, 44 m.p.h.; take-off distance to 35 ft., 820 ft. (assault); 1,750 ft. (long-range); landing distance from 35 ft., 738 ft. to 1,230 ft. (according to mission weight); range, 540 n. miles (assault) to 1,600 n. miles (ferry).

1. *Breguet 940 Integral.*
2. *Breguet 941 in flight.*
3. *Breguet 941 take-off.*
4. *Breguet 941 landing.*

1

2

3

4

CANADAIR CL-41 TUTOR (Canada)

A production model Canadair CT-114 Tutor.

AN R.C.A.F. DECISION in September 1961 placed the Canadair CL-41 in production after the company had spent more than ten years and about $3 million on the design and development of a basic jet trainer.

The CL-41 was laid out along lines similar to those of the Hunting Jet Provost (pp. 71–73), with a low wing, side-by-side seating, bifurcated wing-root air intakes, a single jet pipe and a T-tail. The 2,400 lb.s.t. Pratt & Whitney JTI2A-5 turbojet was selected as the power-plant and the first of two prototypes, CF-LTW-X, made its first flight at Montreal on January 13, 1960. The second prototype was completed but was not flown until 1962, after it had been modified to CL-41R standard as described below.

CL-41A. This company designation distinguishes the production version of the trainer for the R.C.A.F. The type was adopted after extensive demonstration flying by the prototype, and was given the official designation CT-114 Tutor.

The Tutor differs from the original CL-41 in several respects and notably in the changed powerplant, a 2,825 lb.s.t. General Electric CJ610-1B having been substituted for the Pratt & Whitney unit. This engine is built in Canada by Orenda Engines as the J85-CAN-40. To allow early experience to be obtained with the new installation, a U.S.-built J85-GE-7 was fitted in the prototype CF-LTW-X and flight trials in this form were resumed on November 26, 1962. Larger air brakes were introduced at the same time.

Production deliveries of the Tutor began in the latter part of 1963 after an official naming ceremony for the first aircraft on October 29, 1963. The R.C.A.F. order is for 190 aircraft.

CL-41G. This version of the Canadair trainer was projected for the counter-insurgency rôle. It retains most features of the CL-41A, with the addition of armour plate to protect the crew from ground fire. In addition to four strong points beneath the wings to carry up to 3,000 lb. of bombs, missiles, gun pods or other stores, a single pick-up is provided under the fuselage for a 500 lb. bomb. Extra fuel is carried in optional wing-tip tanks. Full training capability is retained.

Canadair built a CL-41G demonstrator (CF-OUM-X) as a private venture during 1964, the first flight being made on June 9, 1964. This was the 15th production CT-114 on temporary loan from the R.C.A.F.

CL-41R. To meet the requirements of air forces using advanced tactical aircraft, the CL-41R was projected as a systems trainer capable of carrying the full range of electronic equipment used in the operational aircraft. To accommodate this equipment, the nose was lengthened by 10 ft. and fairings were added on each side of the fuselage just aft of the wings. Provision was made for two 62 Imp. gallon wing-tip tanks to supplement the 250 Imp. gallon internal capacity.

The second prototype CL-41, CF-LTX-X, was completed as a CL-41R demonstrator and first flew—with Pratt & Whitney JT12 engine—on July 13, 1962. A J85 engine was installed at the end of the same year. This aircraft carries the NASRR equipment but CYRANO or TARAN can also be fitted.

Data for the CT-114 Tutor:
Span, 36 ft. 6 in.; length, 32 ft. 0 in.; height, 9 ft. 2¾ in.; wing area, 220 sq. ft.; aspect ratio, 6.0; sweepback, nil.
Gross weight, 7,390 lb.; zero fuel weight, 5,336 lb.
Max. speed, Mach=0.71 (488 m.p.h. at 30,000 ft.); initial rate of climb, 4,250 ft./min.; service ceiling, 44,500 ft.; take-off distance to 50 ft., 2,100 ft.; landing distance from 50 ft., 2,300 ft.; range (internal fuel, ferry mission), 940 miles; endurance (training mission), 2 hr. 9 min.

1

2

3

4

---

1. *The prototype CL-41, CF-LTW-X.*
2. *The prototype repainted in R.C.A.F. colours.*
3. *The CL-41R, CF-LTX-X.*
4. *The CL-41G, CF-OUM-X.*

CANADAIR CL-44 YUKON (Canada)

CANADAIR LTD. began work in 1956 on the development of a new long-range troop and freight transport to meet a requirement of the Royal Canadian Air Force. At that time, the Canadian company had already obtained—in March 1954—a licence to develop and produce aircraft derived from the Bristol Britannia turboprop transport. One such variant, the CL-28 Argus, had gone into production in the Canadair plant and the Britannia became the starting point of the design for the new transport.

A series of design studies was completed,

1. *The Canadair CL-44 on its first take-off.*
2. *The first CL-44, serial 15501.*
3. *A production model CL-44, serial 15924.*

under the manufacturer's designation of CL-44, in which the Britannia wing was retained with a fuselage having the same cross-section but greater length than that of the British aeroplane.

The Bristol Orion turboprop was chosen to power the CL-44, which the R.C.A.F. ordered in 1958. A few months later, work on the Orion was discontinued as an economy measure by the British government and the CL-44 had to be re-designed to use the 5,730 e.h.p. Rolls-Royce Tyne 515. The military variant with these engines was known as the CL-44-6 and was designated CC-106 Yukon by the R.C.A.F., which later increased its order for this type from eight to twelve.

The CC-106 was procured for use primarily as a long-range cargo carrier, for which purpose it has a number of special features. Two large freight loading doors are provided, one ahead of and one behind the wing.

As a freighter, the Yukon carries a crew of six and a payload of 62,430 lb. It can, alternatively, carry up to 134 passengers with a crew of nine or, in the casualty evacuation version, 80 patients with a crew of nine. A Blackburn Artouste APU is carried in the nose-wheel bay to provide compressed air for main engine starting and ground air conditioning.

The first Yukon made its first flight at Cartierville on November 15, 1959. At this time it carried the serial number 15501, but it was later re-numbered 15932. The first and second aircraft were subsequently fitted out for V.I.P. transport duties with No. 412 Squadron at Ottawa, and were then re-numbered 15555 and 16666. The other ten Yukons went into service with No. 437 Squadron, deliveries being completed in 1961.

Span, 142 ft. 4 in.; length, 136 ft. 10 in.; height, 38 ft. 11 in.; wing area, 2,075 sq. ft.; sweep-back, nil.
Max. gross weight, 205,000 lb.; zero fuel weight, 155,000 lb.; max. payload, 60,763 lb.
Cruising speed, 389 m.p.h.; service ceiling, 26,000 ft.; take-off distance to 50 ft., 6,400 ft.; landing distance from 50 ft., 3,600 ft.; range with max. cargo payload, 3,135 miles; range with max. passengers, 4,260 miles; max. range, 5,757 miles.

C.A.S.A. 1.131 (Spain)

THIS PRE-WAR GERMAN DESIGN, the Bücker 131 Jungmann primary trainer, was still in production in Spain in 1964, and continues to serve the Spanish Air Force (Ejercito del Aire). The Jungmann first flew in Germany in 1934 and was produced in large quantities during the War with a 100 h.p. Hirth Hm 504 engine.

Spanish interest in German aircraft dates from the Civil War, when many of the types then under development for the Luftwaffe were flown operationally in support of General Franco's forces. In 1937, the Spanish Government concluded licence agreements with Germany covering production of the Gotha 145 transition trainer, the Junkers Ju 52/3m tri-motor transport, the Heinkel He 111 bomber, and the Bücker Bu 131 and Bü 133 Jungmeister. All these types were subsequently produced in various of the factories of Construcciones Aeronauticas, S.A., Spain's longest-established aircraft manufacturing concern. After the outbreak of war in 1939 their development in Spain had to proceed using wholly local material and resources.

The Jungmann entered production in the Cadiz plant, which had been set up in 1927 to build seaplanes for the Spanish Air Force and Navy. By 1962, 500 examples had been built under the Spanish designation C1.131E and work was in hand on a final quantity of 25. The C1.131E (designated E-3B by the Spanish Air Force) is powered by a 125 h.p. ENMASA Tigre G.IV—a four-cylinder in-line engine, also built in Spain.

The C1.131E is a conventional biplane of mixed construction with fabric covering. Both the fuselage and the tail unit are metal structures fabricated from metal tubes; the wings are of two-spar wooden construction, with steel interplane struts. Pupil and instructor are seated in tandem in open cockpits, each having their own complete set of flying controls, engine controls and instruments.

Of the 100 Jungmann built by Dornier in Switzerland, a number remain in service with the Swiss Air Force.

In addition to the C1.131Es, C.A.S.A. built 25 Bü 133 Jungmeisters at Cadiz. These went into service with the Spanish Air Force under the designation ES-1, but they are no longer operational. In Switzerland, Dornier built 47 of the radial-engined Jungmeisters, a few of which were still in service in 1964.

Data for the C1.131E:
Span, 24 ft. 3 in.; length, 22 ft. 1 in.; height, 7 ft. 4 in.; wing area, 145.3 sq. ft.; sweep-back, 11 degrees.
Empty weight, 992 lb.; gross weight, 1,587 lb.
Max. speed, 124 m.p.h. at sea level; cruising speed, 98 m.p.h.; initial rate of climb, 1,020 ft./min.; service ceiling, 17,710 ft.; range, 310 miles.

1

2

1, 2 and 3. C.A.S.A.-built Bücker 131s in service with the Spanish Air Force with the designation E3B (C.A.S.A. 1.133E).

3

C.A.S.A. C.207 AZOR (Spain)

Three production models of the C.A.S.A. 207 Azor.

ESTABLISHED IN MARCH 1923 at Getafe, Construcciones Aeronauticas S.A. has been engaged primarily in the production of aircraft built under licence for the Spanish Air Force and Spanish Navy. The first C.A.S.A. product was the Breguet XIX general purpose biplane. Later types which have been produced under licence include the Breguet "Grand Raid" and Breguet 26, Avro and Hawker biplanes, Dornier Wal, Vickers Vildebeest, Heinkel He 111, Junkers Ju 52/3m, Gotha Go 145 and Bücker Bü 131 and Bü 133 (see p. 21).

A design office was established at the C.A.S.A. works in Getafe in 1946, although one original design had already been produced —the C.A.S.A. 111 of 1929. First product of the new design unit was the C.A.S.A. 201 Alcotan, a ten-seat light transport which made its first flight on February 11, 1949. In addition to two prototypes, C.A.S.A. built 110 Alcotans for the Spanish Air Force, which used them in three principal versions—the 201B transport, 201F navigation, radio and multi-engine pilot trainer and the 201G bombing and photographic trainer.

The Alcotan was powered by two 500 h.p. ENMA Sirio VIIA radial engines; also fitted experimentally were two 475 h.p. Cheetah 27s, two 550 h.p. Leonides 503s and two 450 h.p. Wasp Juniors.

From the C.201, C.A.S.A. evolved a slightly larger but similar design, the C.202 Halcon. First flown in May 1952, the Halcon differed from the earlier design by having a nose-wheel undercarriage and was powered by 775 h.p. ENMA Beta B41 radial engines. Seats were provided for 14 passengers in addition to the crew of three.

A batch of 20 C.202s has been built by C.A.S.A. for the Spanish Air Force, with the designation T.5. A single C.202B, flown in 1956, had two Wright Cyclone engines and was furnished as an executive transport.

Third in the series of C.A.S.A. transports designed for the Spanish Air Force, the C.207 Azor first flew on September 28, 1955. Considerably larger than the two earlier types, the C.207 retained the same overall layout, which was that of a conventional low-wing twin-engined monoplane. It provides accommodation for a maximum of 38 equipped troops, or

30–36 passengers, seated three-abreast across the cabin. Twenty-four stretchers can be carried when the aircraft is used for casualty evacuation, and a paratroop version has been designed with an additional door and facilities for 30 paratroops.

A pre-series of ten Azors has been built for the Spanish Air Force, which uses them under the designation T.7 as general purpose transports. A second batch of ten, under production in 1964, are C.207Cs and will be equipped specifically for cargo carrying.

The Azor is powered by two Bristol Hercules 730 engines rated at 2,040 h.p. each.

Data for the Azor:

Span, 91 ft. 2½ in.; length, 68 ft. 5 in.; height, 25 ft. 5 in.; wing area, 923 sq. ft.; sweepback, nil; aspect ratio, 9.

Empty weight, 23,370 lb.; payload, 5,262 lb.; gross weight, 36,375 lb.; max. landing weight, 33,070 lb.

Max. speed, 283 m.p.h. at 6,100 ft.; cruising speed, 249 m.p.h.; service ceiling, 26,250 ft.; range, 1,622 miles; take-off distance to 50 ft., 2,296 ft.; landing distance from 50 ft., 2,231 ft,

1

2

3

4

1. *A C.A.S.A. 201 Alcotan in service markings.*
2, 3 *and* 4. *The prototype C.A.S.A. 207 Azor, XT7-2.*

CESSNA **T-37** (U.S.A.)

A formation of Cessna T-37As in U.S.A.F. service.

CESSNA'S FIRST JET aeroplane, the T-37 is also the first basic jet trainer developed for service with the U. S. Air Force. An invitation to bid for contracts was issued to the U.S. manufacturing industry in April 1952.

The specification was hotly contested. Cessna completed their Model 318 proposal by June 1952 and in December were named winners of the contest. The Cessna aeroplane was a simple low-wing monoplane powered by two Continental J69 (licence-built Turboméca Marboré II) turbojets buried in the thickened wing centre section, with side-by-side seating for pupil and instructor.

Cessna received a contract for three prototypes of their trainer with the U.S.A.F. designation XT-37. The first of these flew on October 12, 1954, powered by YJ69-T-9 engines rated at 920 lb. thrust each. To improve the spin recovery, modifications were made which lengthened the fuselage and enlarged the fin; added a ventral fin and introduced distinctive strakes around the nose.

Thus modified, the T-37 was accepted by the U.S.A.F., which had ordered a development batch of 11 in 1954. Production and experimental models have been produced as follows:

T-37A. Initial production version for U.S.A.F. Consolidated Pilot Training Programme. First flight on September 27, 1955. Deliveries to U.S.A.F. began in 1956 with first training courses in 1957. In November 1958 a training course was started on T-37s from scratch, followed a few months later by a second similar experiment. Subsequently, a training syllabus was established whereby trainees flew 132 hours on the T-37 followed by 130 hours on the Northrop T-38. This was again modified in 1964 when the Cessna T-41 was introduced as a basic trainer (*see* p. 28).

Production of the T-37A totalled 416 and ended in 1959. Three of these aircraft were evaluated in the ground support rôle by the U.S. Army in 1957.

T-37B. Second production version of the Cessna trainer, featuring 1,024 lb.s.t. J69-T-25 engines, giving an increase in top speed from 324 knots to 369 knots. A later standard of equipment was fitted. The T-37B entered production in 1959 and the first was delivered to the U.S.A.F. on November 6 in that year. In addition to new production, all T-37As were cycled through a modification programme to bring them up to T-37B standard.

Foreign countries which received the T-37B included Pakistan, Greece (20), Peru (15) and Thailand (8). By mid-1964, more than 800 T-37s had been built.

T-37C. Primarily for use by foreign nations receiving military aid from the U.S., the T-37C was developed as an armed version of the trainer with underwing pick-up points for various stores and wing-tip tanks for greater range. Cessna conducted flight trials with a T-37C carrying the civil registration N5427E before starting delivery. At least 30 T-37Cs have been supplied to Portugal and four to Vietnam.

T-37D. As part of the U.S.A.F. investigation of aircraft suitable for counter-insurgency duties, two specially modified T-37s have been produced as YAT-37Ds. They have 2,400 lb.s.t. General Electric J85-GE-5 turbojets, a gross weight of 10,500 lb. and six strong points for underwing stores. First flight was made on October 22, 1963.

Data for T-37B:
Span, 33 ft. 9½ in.; length, 29 ft. 3 in.; height, 9 ft. 2 in.; wing area, 184 sq. ft.; aspect ratio, 5.2; sweepback, nil.
Empty weight, 4,056 lb.; gross weight, 6,574 lb.
Max. speed, 425 m.p.h. at 20,000 ft.; cruising speed, 368 m.p.h. at 35,000 ft.; initial climb, 3,370 ft./min.; service ceiling, 38,700 ft.; max. range, 932 miles; take-off to 50 ft., 2,024 ft.; landing distance from 50 ft., 2,600 ft.

1. *The prototype XT-37.*
2. *Cessna T-37B.*
3. *Cessna T-37C trials aircraft with gun pods and tip tanks.*
4. *Cessna YAT-37D counter-insurgency version.*

1

2

3

4

CESSNA O-1 BIRD DOG (U.S.A.)

A Cessna O-1E, U.S. Army.

IN 1949, THE U.S. ARMY drew up a requirement for a two-seat liaison aircraft which would be used for close support of ground troops and artillery units. In late August of that year, the aircraft industry was invited to submit prototype aircraft for a flight evaluation to be held in March 1950.

Cessna Aircraft Company's submission, identified as the Cessna 305, was ready in 90 days and made its first flight in December 1949. Based on the design of the Model 170, the new Cessna 305 had a 210 h.p. Continental engine and high-lift slotted flaps for good field performance.

In competition with three other aircraft, the Cessna 305 emerged the winner in June 1950 and an initial contract was placed for 418 examples designated L-19A. First production model of the L-19A rolled out of the Wichita plant in November 1950 and 100 examples were flying with the U.S. Army in Korea by January 1951. Variants of the series, which were re-designated in the O-1 category in 1961 are as follows:

O-1A (L-19A). The initial (and principal) production version for the U.S. Army. Cessna Model 305A with a 210 h.p. Continental O-470 engine. Of 2,466 built for the U.S. Army, 66 were L-19A-IT instrument trainers with a rear instrument panel, adjustable rear seat and blind flight curtains.

O-1B (OE-1). 60 Bird Dogs for the U.S. Marines, identical with L-19A apart from the exterior finish. The same designation was given to the two Cessna 305Cs (*see* O-1E below) acquired by the U.S. Navy in 1959.

XL-19B. Under a research contract from the U.S.A.F., Cessna installed a Boeing XT50-BO-1 turboprop in an L-19A. It first flew on November 2, 1952.

XL-19C. Two examples powered by a 280 h.p. Continental XT51-T-1 (Turboméca Artouste) turboprop. They first flew, respectively, on September 1, 1953 and June 25, 1954. The XL-19Cs had new fuel tanks of twice the normal capacity and these tanks were retained after the two aircraft were converted back to L-19 standard in 1955.

O-1C (OE-2). Developed L-19A for U.S. Marines with more power. Cessna Model 321, with a 260 h.p. Continental O-470-2, a new fuselage and other changes. The Marines bought 25 (originally designated OE-2) but no Army contracts were placed.

O-1D (TL-19D). For use as instrument trainers, the U.S. Army purchased 307 of this variant in 1956–58. They were similar to the L-19A-IT but had a higher gross weight (2,400 lb.) and a constant speed propeller. Cessna designation was Model 305B.

O-1E (L-19E). New U.S. Army variant in 1956 with minor improvements (Cessna Model 305C). Total Army contracts for 346; delivery began in November 1956. In addition, one L-19E was supplied to the U.S.A.F., nine were ordered by Canada and 75 were purchased for the Mutual Defense Aid Program and supplied to other nations by the U.S. Government. In 1959, production of the L-19E was resumed to build 36 for France, and at this time two others were supplied to the U.S. Navy as OE-1s. The type has also been built by Fuji in Japan.

O-1F. This description applies to examples of the Bird Dog operated on observation duties by the U.S.A.F. in Vietnam.

Data for the O-1E:
Span, 36 ft. 0 in.; length, 25 ft. 9½ in.; height, 7 ft. 3½ in.; wing area, 174 sq. ft.; sweepback, nil.
Empty weight, 1,614 lb.; gross weight, 2,430 lb.
Max. speed, 115 m.p.h.; cruising speed, 104 m.p.h. at 5,000 ft.; initial rate of climb, 1,150 ft./min.; service ceiling, 18,500 ft.; take-off distance to 50 ft., 560 ft.; landing distance from 50 ft., 600 ft.; range, 530 miles.

1. *The Cessna 305 N41694, prototype for the L-19 series.*
2. *Cessna TL-19D instrument trainer in overall orange finish.*
3. *The XL-19B with Boeing XT50 turboprop.*
4. *Cessna O-1C, U.S. Marines.*

CESSNA T-41 and 180 Series (U.S.A.)

WHILST THE MAJORITY of Cessna aircraft built for military liaison and observation duties have been in the Model 305 (O-1 Bird Dog) series as described on pages 26–27, a few examples of other commercial models have been supplied for military use. These include, in particular, the Model 180 and 182 supplied to some Governments overseas, and the Model 172 adopted by the U.S.A.F. as a basic trainer, the T-41.

Fifteen examples of the Cessna 180 four-seat lightplane were acquired by the Australian Army and are used to equip No. 16 Army Light Aircraft Squadron for observation and reconnaissance duties. Other examples of the Cessna 180 are used by the air forces of Austria, Argentine Navy, Indonesia, Korea and Mexico.

---

1. *A Cessna 180 in Royal Australian Army markings.*
2. *A Cessna 182 in service with the Austrian Air Force.*
3. *The first Cessna T-41A.*

Differing from the Model 180 noticeably in having a nose-wheel in place of tail-wheel undercarriage, the Cessna 182 serves with the Canadian Army, which has acquired four examples under the designation L-19L.

Early in 1964, the U.S.A.F. decided to revert to the use of a piston-engined aircraft for basic pilot training, which for several years had been conducted on the Cessna T-37 jet trainer from scratch. Experience showed that pupils unsuitable for training as pilots would not be identified until some way through the training syllabus, leading to considerable waste of money. Use of a simpler basic or *ab initio* trainer makes it possible to spot unsuitable pupils at an earlier stage and avoids giving them expensive training on the jet types.

As a consequence of this decision, the U.S.A.F. announced that it would select a suitable light aircraft for use as a basic trainer and would order these "off-the-shelf". From several designs submitted, the Cessna 172 was chosen in July 1964 and was designated the T-41A. A fixed-price contract for 170 examples was placed and the first example of a Cessna 172 in U.S.A.F. markings was flying by September 1964.

Operational use of the T-41As began early in 1965, with delivery of the entire batch of 170 scheduled to be complete by July 1965. Under the new U.S.A.F. syllabus, pupils receive some 30 hours flight instruction on the T-41A, prior to going on to the Cessna T-37B.

This phase of U.S.A.F. pilot training is being handled by civilian contractors located close to the Air Force Bases where the T-37Bs are in use. Eight T-41As have been purchased by Ecuador.

The following data refers to the civilian model of the Cessna 172, over 10,000 examples of which have been sold since 1955.

Span, 36 ft. 2 in.; length, 26 ft. 6 in.; height, 8 ft. 11 in.; wing area, 175 sq. ft.; aspect ratio, 7.52; sweepback, nil.
Empty weight, 1,260 lb.; gross weight, 2,250 lb.
Max. speed, 139 m.p.h.; cruising speed, 100 m.p.h.; initial rate of climb, 700 ft./min.; service ceiling, 14,550 ft.; take-off distance to 50 ft., 1,430 ft.; landing distance from 50 ft., 1,140 ft.; range, 650 miles.

CESSNA U-17 and SKYWAGON (U.S.A.)

ONE OF THE LARGEST aircraft in the Cessna single-engined range, the Model 185 Skywagon appeared in March 1961. It was intended to meet the requirements of "bush" flying in export markets outside the U.S.A. and for a rugged utility aircraft in the domestic market.

Powered by a 260 h.p. Continental IO-470 engine, the Model 185 was based on the Cessna 180 but was structurally re-designed to carry greater payloads at higher speeds. It seats six and has a useful load which is greater than its empty equipped weight. A glass-fibre Cargo-Pack, with 300 lb. capacity, can be carried under the fuselage to increase the Skywagon's versatility.

Orders were placed, soon after the type had been announced, by the South African Air Force for 25 and by the Peruvian Air Force for nine.

Subsequently, the U.S. Air Force ordered a batch of 25 Skywagons under the designation U-17A, to be supplied to other nations under the U.S. Military Assistance Program. Further contracts placed for U-17As for M.A.P. use brought the total on order to 141 by January, 1965.

Among the nations which have received U-17As are Costa Rica, whose Civil Guard has three; Laos and South Vietnam. In Vietnam the U-17As were reported to be dropping five-man "harassment teams" behind the lines in North Vietnam, having presumably been modified for para-dropping.

Span, 36 ft. 2 in.; length, 25 ft. 6 in.; height, 7 ft. 7 in.; wing area, 175 sq. ft.; aspect ratio, 7.52; sweepback, nil.
Empty weight, 1,580 lb.; gross weight, 3,200 lb.
Max. speed, 176 m.p.h.; cruising speed, 133 m.p.h.; initial rate of climb, 1,000 ft./min.; service ceiling, 17,300 ft.; take-off distance to 50 ft., 1,510 ft.; landing distance from 50 ft., 1,265 ft.; range, 700–900 miles.

1. *A commercial Cessna Skywagon, similar to the U-17A.*
2. *Skywagons in the markings of the Peruvian Air Force.*

CESSNA U-3 and SKYKNIGHT (U.S.A.)

ONE OF THE BEST KNOWN "light twins" in the U.S.A., the Cessna 310 originated in 1951 and a prototype first flew on January 3, 1953. Certification was obtained in March 1954 and production deliveries began later the same year.

Late in 1956, when the U.S. Air Force formulated a requirement for a light twin-engined communications aircraft to be bought "off-the-shelf" the Cessna 310 was one of the types evaluated. Emerging as the winner of this evaluation, the 310 was ordered for U.S.A.F. use, receiving the official designation L-27A and a contract for 80. For the first time in U.S.A.F. history, the equipment to be used in the new aircraft was selected entirely from that optionally offered on the commercial version; the only new features were auxiliary fuel tanks, a new instrument panel, special uphol-stery and regulation U.S.A.F. external finish.

Another innovation was the method adopted for logistics support. In place of setting up its own spares support for the L-27A, the U.S.A.F. agreed to make use of the existing Cessna commercial dealer organization for parts and components needed for maintenance.

Delivery of the L-27As began in May 1957 and was completed in December. A second batch of 80 was delivered to U.S.A.F. between May and November 1958. These aircraft were later re-designated U-3As in the Utility category; to those who fly them they are usually known as the Blue Canoe (the external colours are blue and white) or the U-Bird.

Final U.S.A.F. procurement of this type occurred in 1961 when 35 U-3Bs were pur-chased. Identified by Cessna as Model 310E, these were identical with the commercial Model 310F. This variant sported a sweptback fin and rudder and an additional set of rear windows; the U-3B had Air Force radio and a few items of special equipment.

Air Force U-3s are used for a variety of missions, including communications flights for personnel and logistics flights with light cargo, aerial survey operations and instrument and navigation procedure training and check flying.

The U-3 is exclusively a U.S.A.F. aircraft, but a few other examples of the Cessna twin have gone into military service elsewhere. In particular, Peru acquired two Cessna 320 Skyknights for use as executive transports and on liaison duties. The Skyknight is basically a supercharged version of the Cessna 310.

Examples of the Cessna 310 are used by the Air Forces of Argentina and Malaysia, amongst others.

Data for the U-3B:
Span, 36 ft. 11 in.; length, 29 ft. 7 in.; height, 9 ft. 11¼ in.; wing area, 175 sq. ft.; aspect ratio, 7.3; sweepback, nil.
Empty weight, 3,045 lb.; gross weight, 4,990 lb.
Max. speed, 239 m.p.h.; cruising speed, 218 m.p.h. at 8,000 ft.; initial rate of climb, 1,750 ft./min.; service ceiling, 20,700 ft.; take-off distance to 50 ft., 1,470 ft.; landing distance from 50 ft., 1,770 ft.; range, over 1,300 miles with auxiliary tanks.

---

1. *A Cessna Skyknight in the markings of the Peruvian Air Force.*
2. *Cessna U-3A of the U.S. Air Force.*
3. *Cessna U-3B.*

DE HAVILLAND CV-7 BUFFALO (Canada)

THE DE HAVILLAND AIRCRAFT of Canada Ltd. has been responsible for the production of a series of "bush" aircraft and larger transports which, in addition to commanding orders from a variety of commercial operators, have met the more specialized requirements of the U.S. Army. In chronological order, these types have included the Beaver, Otter and Caribou (see pp. 32–37); the latest in the series is the Buffalo.

Design proposals for a new STOL tactical transport were invited by the U.S. Army in May 1962, with 25 companies being invited to submit designs. One of the principal requirements was that the new aircraft should be compatible with the CH-47 Chinook helicopter in terms of load. This meant that it would have to carry a payload of about 5 tons and be able to accommodate all the components of the Pershing missile system; a 105 mm. howitzer; a ¾-ton truck or 40 equipped troops. Loads delivered to forward airfields by the new tactical transport could then be ferried on to the battle zone by helicopters without re-assembly and sub-division.

A developed version of the de Havilland Caribou was the winner of the Army competition. Its principal new features were an enlarged fuselage, higher operating weights and two 2,850 h.p. General Electric T64-GE-10 turboprops. At the time the design of the DHC-5 Caribou II (as the project was at first known) was being completed, de Havilland had already gained preliminary experience of the T64 engine by modifying the prototype Caribou to have this powerplant. In this form it first flew on September 22, 1961.

For evaluation and prototype development, the U.S. Army ordered four prototypes of the new design, to be jointly financed by the makers, the Canadian Government and the Army. These aircraft were at first designated YAC-2, this being later changed to YCV-7A. The name Buffalo is a de Havilland choice and may not be retained by the U.S. Army. First flight of the YCV-7A was made on April 9, 1964. Fifteen Buffaloes were ordered for the R.C.A.F. at the end of 1964, and the first CV-7A was delivered to the U.S. Army in April 1965.

Span, 96 ft. 0 in.; length, 77 ft. 4 in.; height, 28 ft. 8 in.; wing area, 945 sq. ft.; aspect ratio, 9.75; sweepback, nil.
Empty weight, 23,370 lb.; max. payload, 10,630 lb.; gross weight, 41,000 lb.; max. landing weight, 36,500 lb.
Max. speed, 267 m.p.h. at 10,000 ft.; cruising speed, 198 m.p.h. at 10,000 ft.; initial rate of climb, 1,950 ft./min.; service ceiling, 29,000 ft.; take-off distance to 50 ft., 1,225 ft.; landing distance from 50 ft., 1,100 ft.; range, 530 miles.

1

2

3

1. *The prototype Caribou re-engined with T64 turboprops.*
2. *The first Buffalo landing.*
3. *An air-to-air view of the second Buffalo.*

DE HAVILLAND **CV-2 CARIBOU** (Canada)

A Caribou in the markings of the Royal Australian Air Force.

AS A FURTHER STAGE in the evolution of a successful range of light and medium transports with STOL capability and rugged "workhorse" qualities, de Havilland Aircraft of Canada embarked upon the design of a twin-engined transport in 1956. This step followed two years of study into the possibilities of combining the load-carrying ability of the DC-3 with the STOL performance of the Beaver and Otter (*see* pp. 34–37).

The new design was seen initially as a "twin Otter" but this concept was soon left behind and the DHC-4 evolved as a completely new aircraft and the largest in the range, with a gross weight of 26,000 lb. A high-wing layout was adopted, with anhedral between the fuselage and engine nacelles to bring the latter as close to the ground as practical in order to shorten the undercarriage. A single rear loading ramp was built into the rear fuselage, under the tall single fin and rudder. Two 1,450 h.p. Pratt & Whitney R-2000-7M2 engines were chosen, these being of the same type already employed in the Douglas DC-4.

With the design firmly established, de Havilland obtained the support of the Canadian Government with an order for one example to be used by the Royal Canadian Air Force, plus co-operation of the Canadian Department of Defence Production in construction of a prototype. An order for five examples was then placed by the U.S. Army, in 1957, for evaluation and work on the batch of seven aircraft including a prototype went ahead.

First flight of the prototype Caribou was made on July 30, 1958 and the first for the U.S. Army followed in March 1959. The Army designation was AC-1 (later changed to CV-2) and the first three YAC-1s were handed over on October 8, 1959. Evaluation trials began immediately but even before these had been completed, an initial production order was placed, for seven aircraft. Subsequent contracts have brought the sale of Caribou to the U.S. Army to a total of 159, with deliveries continuing into 1964. These aircraft are of two types, the CV-2A with a gross weight of 26,000 lb. and the CV-2B at 28,500 lb. with minor changes.

A wide variety of military stores could be carried in the fuselage of the Caribou, making up the maximum payload of four tons. The loads can include two Army jeeps, or 32 troops in wall-type folding seats, or 24 fully-equipped paratroopers or 20 standard Army litters with four seats for other patients or attendants. The rear loading ramp can be adjusted to match the truck bed height of a vehicle backed up to the door and the ramp and rear door can be opened in flight to drop paratroops or supplies. A mechanical freight handling system can be installed and four 1,500 lb. freight pallets can be carried. These also can be para-dropped from the rear doors.

In addition to the U.S. Army, several other air arms have purchased the Caribou. The R.C.A.F. purchased a further eight, of which four were assigned to the United Nations forces in the Middle East. Other contracts for the Caribou have come from the Ghana Air Force (8), the Kuwait Air Force (2), the Indian Air Force (16) and the Royal Australian Air Force (18). One was acquired for evaluation in Sweden and others have been ordered by the Kenya and Zambia Air Forces.

Span, 75 ft. 7½ in.; length, 72 ft. 7 in.; height, 31 ft. 9 in.; wing area, 912 sq. ft.; aspect ratio, 10; sweepback, nil.
Empty weight 18,260 lb.; payload, 8,740 lb.; gross weight, 28,500 lb. (31,300 lb. for ferry missions).
Max. speed, 216 m.p.h. at 6,500 ft.; cruising speed, 182 m.p.h. at 7,500 ft.; initial rate of climb, 1,355 ft./min.; service ceiling, 24,800 ft.; take-off distance to 50 ft., 1,185 ft.; landing distance from 50 ft., 1,235 ft.; range, 242 miles (1,300 miles with max. fuel).

1. *A Caribou prototype, CF-LKF-X, in U.S. Army colours.*
2. *One of the R.C.A.F. Caribou allocated to the United Nations.*
3. *The Caribou for evaluation by the Swedish Army and Air Force.*
4. *Kuwait Air Force markings on the Caribou.*

DE HAVILLAND **OTTER** (Canada)

An R.C.A.F. Otter in Rescue markings, with amphibious floats.

OF APPROXIMATELY 450 Otters built by de Havilland Aircraft of Canada up to mid-1964, well over half have been supplied for military duties with at least ten nations. Development of the Otter began in 1950 as a DH private venture following the successful introduction into service of the Beaver (*see* pp. 36–37). It was designed along similar lines, with a single engine, a high wing and a tail-wheel undercarriage, in order to offer the same rugged qualities and STOL performance.

The prototype Otter first flew on December 12, 1951 and the first customer for the military version was the Royal Canadian Air Force. Ultimate procurement of the Otter by the R.C.A.F. totalled 66, and these are used for a variety of tasks including search and rescue duties in the Arctic, paratroop dropping and aerial survey. Some of the R.C.A.F. Otters have also been allocated for duty overseas as part of the R.C.A.F. contribution to the United Nations.

One of the R.C.A.F. Otters has been used since 1957 for an extensive series of flight tests in advanced STOL techniques. These tests have covered three configurations: first, deflected slipstream with large "bat wing" flaps on the inner wing; secondly with the addition of a J85 turbojet in the rear fuselage for inflight reverse thrust and thirdly with two wing-mounted Pratt & Whitney PT6 turboprops in place of the standard R-1340 radial in the nose.

During 1953, de Havilland demonstrated an Otter to the U.S. Army. In a large scale exercise, the Otter demonstrated its ability to operate with substantial loads from small, unprepared fields, and it was selected for large-scale procurement as a new utility transport. Six aircraft for service trials were designated YU-1s by the Army and were delivered in March 1955. They were finished in the white and red markings adopted for aircraft serving in Alaska, and after evaluation they were assigned to U.S. Army units responsible for topographical duties in Alaska—where their ability to operate on skis and floats as well as wheels proved invaluable.

Deliveries of production model U-1As to Army units began in 1956 and more than 150 were purchased. Equipping Army Aviation Transport Companies and finished in drab olive overall, these U-1As provided a new standard of tactical mobility for the U.S. Army, and influenced all subsequent planning for the deployment of both fixed-wing aircraft and helicopters.

Otters have been ordered for service with a number of other air forces, including those of Australia, Burma, Chile, Colombia, Ghana, India, Indonesia and Norway. They serve these air forces as general purpose transports and for more specialized rôles including the dropping of paratroops and supplies. Double doors in the port fuselage side can be completely removed to give an opening 46½ in. wide and ten fully-equipped paratroops can be carried.

The Otter's cabin is 16½ ft. long with a 5 ft. square cross-section. This provides space for nine passenger seats (with a tenth alongside the pilot) or 345 cu. ft. of cargo space when the passenger seats are folded alongside the cabin walls. A 27-in. diameter hatch in the rear of the cabin can be used for cargo and supply dropping or as a position for a survey camera. In the ambulance rôle, the Otter can carry six stretchers plus three passengers in the cabin.

A small number of Otters, purchased by the U.S. Navy, were designated UC-1s. A single example was acquired by the Royal Air Force to accompany the Trans-Antarctic Expedition.

Span, 58 ft.; length, 41 ft. 10 in.; height, 12 ft. 7 in.; wing area, 375 sq. ft.; aspect ratio, 8.97; sweepback, nil.
Empty weight, 4,431 lb.; gross weight, 8,000 lb.
Max. speed, 160 m.p.h. at 5,000 ft.; cruising speed, 121 m.p.h. at sea level; initial rate of climb, 850 ft./min.; service ceiling, 18,800 ft.; take-off distance to 50 ft., 1,155 ft.; landing distance from 50 ft., 880 ft.; range, 875 miles with 2,100 lb. payload.

1. *One of the six YU-1 trials aircraft, in Arctic colours.*
2. *The standard U.S. Army olive finish on a U-1A.*
3. *Indian Air Force Otter.*
4. *Otter for Chile.*

1

2

3

4

DE HAVILLAND **BEAVER** (Canada)

A de Havilland Beaver operated by the Royal Netherlands Air Force.

FIRST FLOWN in August 1947, the Beaver was the second original product of the de Havilland Aircraft of Canada Ltd., the first having been the Chipmunk trainer. With the Beaver, de Havilland broke new ground, setting out to design an aircraft suitable for operation in the Canadian "bush" areas.

Stretching over thousands of square miles above and below the Arctic circle, these areas comprise rugged, often snow-covered, wooded terrain and innumerable waterways and lakes which are frozen solid for much of the year. Since aircraft can play an important rôle in the development of these areas, the provision of suitable "bush" flying aircraft has always proved a challenge to Canadian aircraft designers. Accepting this challenge, de Havilland produced in the Beaver an aircraft not only well-suited to operations in the Canadian outback but one with world-wide appeal as a small utilitarian transport.

The Beaver formula was simple and straightforward—a single, well-proven radial engine (the 450 h.p. Pratt & Whitney R-985 Wasp Junior), a braced, high-mounted wing, single fin and rudder, sturdy, fixed taildown undercarriage and a square section fuselage. Structure was metal throughout.

To cope with any local conditions, the Beaver can operate with a conventional wheel undercarriage, as a floatplane, with amphibious floats, as a skiplane or with combination ski-wheels, selected from the cockpit. The cabin normally provides seats for the pilot and six passengers in a 2:2:3 arrangement. Seats can be quickly removed for freight carrying, and a large loading door is provided on each side of the cabin, in addition to pilot's doors on both sides. Two stretchers can be carried together with three seats in the cabin.

Up to the middle of 1964, just over 1,500 Beavers had been produced, and nearly 1,000 of these had been supplied to the U.S. armed forces. The Beaver won a U.S.A.F./Army design competition for a new liaison aircraft which was held early in 1951 after six examples had been ordered for evaluation—four by the U.S.A.F. and two by the Army. These aircraft, designated YL-20s, were delivered in 1950.

The success of the service trials with these aircraft led to a decision by the U.S. Army to purchase the type in quantity—only the second non-U.S. design to be so favoured since the end of World War II. Initially designated L-20A and subsequently U-6A, the Beavers were used for general liaison, transport and ambulance duties by the Army Air Corps, and saw operational service in the Korean War. They frequently carried an auxiliary fuel tank beneath the fuselage.

L-20As also served with the U.S.A.F. in all its operating theatres from 1953 onwards. Just over 200 went into U.S.A.F. service including 58 with Strategic Air Command; these were usually operated in natural metal finish whereas the Army U-6s were drab olive.

The British Army selected the DHC-2 as standard liaison and light transport equipment in 1960 and ordered 36 to be designated Beaver A.L. Mk.1. Many other nations have purchased the Beaver for military use, including Argentina, Australia, Austria, Cambodia, Dominica, Finland, Ghana, Laos, Muscat and Oman, the Netherlands, Peru, Vietnam, Yugoslavia and Zambia.

Span, 48 ft.; length, 30 ft. 4 in.; height, 9 ft.; wing area, 250 sq. ft.; aspect ratio, 9.2; sweepback, nil.
Empty weight, 3,000 lb.; gross weight, 5,100 lb.
Max. speed, 140 m.p.h. at sea level; cruising speed, 125 m.p.h.; initial rate of climb, 1,020 ft./min.; service ceiling, 18,000 ft.; take-off distance to 50 ft., 1,015 ft.; landing distance from 50 ft., 1,000 ft.; range, 483 miles with full payload.

1. *A production L-20A in U.S.A.F. markings.*
2. *A R.N.Z.A.F. Beaver on skis, accompanying the 1958 Transarctic Expedition.*
3. *Austrian Air Force Beaver.*
4. *Combination wheel-skis on a British Army Beaver.*

DINFIA HUANQUERO and GUARANI (Argentina)

The prototype Guarani II with its distinctive swept-back fin.

THE MAJOR PART of Argentina's aircraft industry is centred on the State-owned and operated DINFIA—the Direccion Nacional de Fabricaciones e Investigaciones Aeronauticas.

DINFIA now operates a number of factories of which the most important is at Cordoba. There, in 1950, work began on a twin-engined general purpose aeroplane to meet Argentine Air Force requirements for a crew trainer and transport. This work gave rise to a successful family of designs which have continued in production up to the present day as the IA35 Huanquero and IA50 Guarani. The prototype IA35 made its first flight on September 21, 1953 and the first of 100 production models flew on March 29, 1957. The variants which have subsequently appeared include the following:

IA35 Huanquero Type 1A. Advanced pilot and navigation trainer, with accommodation for two pilots, a radio operator, instructor and four pupils. Powered by two 620 h.p. IA 19R El Indio engines.

IA35 Huanquero Type 1B. Equipped for bombardier and gunnery training, with two 12.7 mm. Browning guns, internal stowage for four 50-kg. or two 100-kg. bombs and underwing racks for two 5-in. or eight 2.25-in. rockets. Equipment for navigation training is deleted. Powered by two 750 h.p. 1A-R-19-SR1 engines.

IA35 Huanquero Type II. A single example completed in 1955 for use as a light transport carrying a crew of three and seven passengers. Wing tip fuel tanks fitted, plus provision for underwing pylons for supply packs.

IA35 Huanquero Type III. An ambulance version, with provision for four stretchers and an attendant, in addition to the flight crew of three. Engines as Type 1A.

IA35 Huanquero Type IV. Photographic survey variant, carrying a Fairchild 225 camera. Engines as Type 1A.

IA35 Constancia I. A conversion of the third production Huanquero (LQ-FMA) for use as an executive transport version by the Fuerza Aerea Argentina (Argentine Air Force). The design of this conversion was the work of Captain Ing. Hector Eduardo Ruiz, who subsequently became responsible for development of the Guarani described below.

IA35 Pandora. Another transport derivative of the Huanquero, first flown on May 28, 1960. Intended for the civilian market, the Pandora offered accommodation for ten passengers.

IA50 Guarani I. Using the Huanquero design as a basis, Captain Ing. Hector Eduardo Ruiz developed the Guarani as a twin-turboprop executive transport for military or civil use. Powered by two 850 s.h.p. Turboméca Bastan IIIA turboprops, the Guarani I (originally Constancia II) made its first flight on February 6, 1962, bearing the registration letters LQ-HER.

IA50 Guarani II. Improved production model, with a single, sweptback fin and rudder and a shorter rear fuselage, to improve handling and reduce weight. Two 930 s.h.p. Bastan VIA turboprops. Prototype (LV-X27) made its first flight on April 23, 1963, and was to be followed by two pre-production aircraft in 1964. A preliminary production order was placed by the Argentine Air Force for 17 examples of the Guarani II. The data which follow are for Guarani II.

Span, 64 ft. 1 in.; length, 48 ft. 9 in.; height, 19 ft. 0¾ in.; wing area, 450 sq. ft.; aspect ratio, 9; sweepback, nil.
Empty weight, 8,650 lb.; max. payload, 2,600 lb.; max. gross weight, 15,700 lb.; max. landing weight, 13,800 lb.
Max. speed, 310 m.p.h.; cruising speed, 280 m.p.h.; initial rate of climb, 2,640 ft./min.; service ceiling, 41,000 ft.; take-off distance to 50 ft., 2,200 ft.; landing distance from 50 ft., 1,970 ft.; range with max. payload, 1,240 miles.

---

1 and **2.** Two views of the I.A.35 Constancia II, an executive transport version of the Huanquero.
3. The Guarani I, with twin fins and rudders.
4. The Guarani II at Cordoba.

DORNIER **DO 27** (Germany)

A Dornier Do 27 in Luftwaffe colours.

HOLDER OF ONE of the best-known names in German aircraft manufacturing circles, Professor Claude Dornier established a design office in Madrid in 1945 when the design and production of aircraft was forbidden in Germany. The first product of this design unit was a general purpose monoplane of notably clean design, featuring a cantilever high wing and cantilever main wheel oleo legs.

Designated Do 25, a prototype of this design was built for the Oficinas Technicas Dornier by Construcciones Aeronauticas S.A. (C.A.S.A.) and made its first flight on June 25, 1954. The Do 25 was powered by a 150 h.p. E.N.M.A. Tigre G-IVB and was designed to have particularly good low speed characteristics, with double-slotted flaps interconnected with the ailerons and full span leading-edge slots. The large cabin was provided with liberal windows all round for good visibility and had a cargo loading door on each side at the rear.

The Do 25 coincided with a Spanish Air Force requirement and production orders were placed with C.A.S.A. for a developed version designated the Do 27. This had a 275 h.p. Lycoming GO-480 engine giving a general improvement in performance and a number of detail refinements. The undercarriage legs were faired and the external fuel tanks under the wings were replaced by internal tanks.

The prototype Do 27 built by C.A.S.A. first flew on June 27, 1955. Thereafter, Dornier-Werke G.m.b.H. was re-established in Germany and production of the Do 27 began, to meet orders from the Luftwaffe and other customers. C.A.S.A. continued production under licence in Spain to meet Spanish Air Force contracts for 100. These are designated C.A.S.A. C.127s (L-9 by the Spanish Air Force) and the first flew on December 3, 1959.

In Germany, the first Do 27 flew on October 17, 1956. The major production version was designated Do 27A and contracts for this type included one for 428 aircraft from the Luftwaffe, which selected it as the basic communication and liaison type when post-War re-equipment of the German Air Force began.

The Do 27A is equipped to operate in the liaison, observation, ambulance and rescue rôles. Dual control can be fitted to permit its use as a trainer, when the designation is Do 27B. The cabin seats two pilots or pilot and passenger side-by-side and can accommodate up to six more passengers on two bench-type seats running fore-and-aft behind the pilots and facing each other. As well as the doors on each side of the rear passenger compartment, there are doors on each side of the cockpit and another giving access to the baggage compartment in the port side behind the cabin. The cabin floor incorporates a trapdoor which provides a suitable position for an air survey camera.

For heavy freight carrying the cabin floor of the Do 27 can be reinforced. Provision is also made for agricultural spraying and dusting gear to be fitted. As an ambulance, two stretchers can be carried.

In addition to the large orders for Do 27s from the Luftwaffe and the Spanish Air Force, the type has been purchased in smaller quantities by several other air forces. Seven have been acquired for use by the Royal Swedish Army and a similar number by the Swiss Air Force. Two went into service in 1962 with the South African Air Force. Dual-control Do 27Bs were chosen by the embryo Federal Nigerian Air Force for use as trainers in 1963, and a few others served with the Congolese Air Forces.

Span, 39 ft. 4½ in.; length, 31 ft. 6 in.; height, 9 ft. 2 in.; wing area, 209 sq. ft.; aspect ratio, 7.4; sweepback, nil.
Empty weight, 2,490 lb.; gross weight, 4,070 lb.
Max. speed, 141 m.p.h.; cruising speed, 109 m.p.h.; initial rate of climb, 650 ft./min.; service ceiling, 10,825 ft.; take-off distance to 50 ft., 785 ft.; landing distance from 50 ft., 640 ft.; max. range, 685 miles.

1. *The prototype Do 27, EC-AKY, built in Spain.*
2. *German Air Force Do 27A-4 at take-off.*
3. *Olive and grey colours of the German Air Force on a Do 27.*
4. *Built by C.A.S.A. for the Spanish Air Force, a C-127.*

DOUGLAS C-133 CARGOMASTER (U.S.A.)

A TOP POLICY decision by the U.S.A.F. in 1951 led to the development of new transport aircraft powered by turboprop engines. One of the trio of types then initiated was a heavy strategic freighter capable of transporting all but a small percentage of the Army's field force vehicles fully assembled, and a wide range of missile systems.

A design competition for this freighter was won by the Douglas Aircraft Co. with their DTS-1333 submission. Detail design began in February 1933 under the official title of Logistic Carrier Supporting System SS402L and a production contract was placed in 1954 for 35 aircraft designated C-133A. No prototypes were ordered.

At the time of its inception, the C-133 was the largest military freighter. Its layout followed

---

1. *The first C-133A with original rear fuselage shape.*
2. *A C-133B in M.A.T.S. insignia.*
3. *A late production C-133A in flight.*

the pattern set by the smaller Lockheed Hercules and helped to establish what has become the conventional shape for military freighters in the 'sixties. The main features of this layout are a high wing with four turboprop engines, low floor for direct loading at truck-bed height, rear-loading doors and ramp; and fuselage-side blisters to contain the main undercarriage without interfering with the inside contours of the cabin. Douglas chose the Pratt & Whitney T34 engines to power the C-133.

The production line of C-133As was established at Long Beach and the first aircraft was completed and rolled-out in Febrary 1956, the first flight following on April 23. Initial production aircraft were used for flight testing, leading to changes introduced on the eighth and subsequent C-133A. These changes included a larger dorsal fin and re-contouring the rear fuselage to introduce a flat "beaver tail" shape for better airflow. Early aircraft had T34-P-3 engines but the 6,500 e.s.h.p. T34-P-7 or 7,000 e.s.h.p. (wet rating) T34-P-7A were introduced later, allowing the gross weight to increase from 255,000 lb. to 282,000 lb. Deliveries to the U.S.A.F. began on August 29, 1957.

The Cargomaster's 13,000 cu. ft. cabin could accommodate many missiles complete, but the Titan ICBM was just too long. A modification on the final three C-133As introduced clam-shell loading doors and added 3 ft. to the usable hold length. This same modification applied to the 15 C-133Bs which had 7,500 e.s.h.p. (wet rating) T34-P-9W engines and a gross weight of 286,000 lb.

The first C-133B flew on October 31, 1959 and deliveries began on March 21, 1960.

Data for the C-133B:
Span, 179 ft. 8 in.; length, 157 ft. 6½ in.; height, 48 ft. 3 in.; wing area, 2,673 sq. ft.; aspect ratio, 12.1; sweepback, nil.
Empty equipped weight, 120,363 lb.; gross weight, 286,000 lb.
Max. speed, 359 m.p.h.; cruising speed, 328 m.p.h.; initial rate of climb, 1,280 ft./min.; service ceiling, 20,950 ft.; range, 2,300 miles with max. cargo and 4,400 miles with max. fuel.

FAIRCHILD C-123 PROVIDER (U.S.A.)

IN SERVICE SINCE 1955 with U.S.A.F. Tactical Air Command, the Fairchild C-123 played an important rôle in operation in South Vietnam, where its ability to operate from small unprepared fields proved of significant advantage. Its design originated in the Chase XG-20 cargo glider of 1949, which was itself a development of the wartime XCG-14 and XCG-18 designs.

The all-metal XG-20 was designed from the outset to be adaptable as a powered assault transport and one of the two prototypes was modified to the XC-123 configuration by installation of two Pratt & Whitney R-2800-83 piston engines in wing nacelles. In this form it first flew on October 14, 1949.

The Chase company, responsible for the design of the aircraft, received a contract for five pre-production models designated C-123B, but the company did not have adequate resources to undertake large scale production. Consequently, the Kaiser-Frazer Corporation acquired a controlling interest in Chase in 1953, and the U.S.A.F. then awarded the company a contract for 300 to be built at the Willow Run factory.

After the five pre-production aircraft had been built, the Kaiser-Frazer company ran into financial difficulties and the U.S.A.F. cancelled the contract for C-123s on June 24, 1953. Other companies were invited to bid for the work, and in this Fairchild Engine and Airplane Corp. was successful, receiving the contract later in 1953.

In the light of flight trials with the pre-production aircraft, Fairchild introduced several modifications, mostly of a minor nature but including a large dorsal fin. The first aircraft to the new standard built by Fairchild flew on September 1, 1954, and production totalled 300, including six supplied to the Royal Saudi Air Force and 18 to the Venezuelan Air Force.

The C-123B Provider could accommodate up to 61 equipped troops, 50 stretchers or vehicles with loadings of up to 7,500 lb. per wheel, such as a 155 mm. howitzer and truck. A loading ramp was provided in the rear underside of the fuselage, and doors on each side at the rear could be used by paratroops.

Experience with the C-123Bs in South

Vietnam led to trials in 1962 with a STOL version designated YC-123H. This featured a General Electric CJ610 turbojet in a pod under each wing plus a tail braking parachute and larger wheels and tyres. This reduced the take-off distance needed to clear 50 ft. to below 1,000 ft. with a 6,000 lb. payload and boosted the payload to 20,000 lb.

Span, 110 ft. 0 in.; length, 75 ft. 9 in.; height, 34 ft. 1 in.; wing area, 1,223 sq. ft.; aspect ratio, 9.89; sweepback, nil.
Empty weight, 29,900 lb.; gross weight, 71,000 lb.
Max. speed, 245 m.p.h.; cruising speed, 205 m.p.h.; initial rate of climb, 1,150 ft./min.; service ceiling, 29,000 ft.; range, 1,470 miles with 16,000 lb. payload.

1. *The first Fairchild-built C-123B.*
2. *A Venezualan Air Force C-123B.*
3. *A C-123B operating with Tactical Air Force, U.S.A.F.*

FOKKER F 27M TROOPSHIP (Netherlands)

A Fokker F2 7M Troopship of the Royal Netherlands Air Force.

PRIMARILY A COMMERCIAL light transport for airline use, the Fokker F 27 Friendship has also been supplied in small numbers for military use. The majority of those in use with air forces are the F 27M model which incorporates a number of special features. A few examples of the commercial F 27 are also in military service.

The F 27 originated with design studies made in 1950 in the general field of a "DC 3 replacement". These led, by 1953, to a final proposal for a twin-Dart feeder-liner; prototypes were built with financial backing from the Netherlands Government and the first of these flew on November 24, 1955. Production lines were established in the Fokker works at Schiphol, Amsterdam, and by Fairchild at Hagerstown in the U.S. Deliveries from these two lines began in 1958.

The eleventh F 27 from the Fokker production line was delivered in September 1959 to the Philippine Air Force for use as a V.I.P. transport. This was the first F 27 delivered in military markings. An order for 12 F 27s for the Royal Netherlands Air Force followed, three of these also being personnel transports to the same general standard as the airline F 27. The remining nine aircraft for the R.Neth.A.F. were to the new F 27M standard.

For military use, the F 27M incorporates a large freight-loading door in the forward fuselage, measuring 91½ in. by 70 in. This door hinges up and opens through a maximum arc of 170 degrees for overhead crane loading.

To allow the F 27M to be used for paratroop dropping, two additional doors are located at the rear of the fuselage, one each side. Measuring 47 in. by 65 in. these doors open inwards and slide away to provide completely clear openings and both doors can be opened simultaneously.

A heavy duty floor is provided in the F 27M, with skid strips running the length of the cabin, and transverse skid strips in the area of the cargo door. Tie down fittings are provided in the floor and along the sides of the cabin beneath the window line. Optional heavy duty lashing rings can be fitted, to withstand loads of up to 15,000 lb. each.

Hat racks are normally retained in the F 27M, but can be folded up to the side wall, when they serve to protect the air conditioning ducts and air outlets from heavy freight. When used as a paratrooper, the F 27M has 45 canvas troop seats installed along either side of the cabin.

For medical evacuation duties, the F 27M can carry 24 stretchers arranged in three tiers down each side of the cabin. Eight canvas seats are provided for sitting casualties or attendants.

A number of special features developed for airline F 27s are also applicable to the F 27M. These include underwing pylon tanks of 200 Imp. gallons capacity each, weather radar in the nose and an optional station for a third member of the flight crew (radio operator/navigator) in the main cabin.

The F 27M is normally powered by two 1,910 s.h.p. Rolls-Royce Dart R.Da.7 engines; these can also be operated at a military rating of 2,210 s.h.p.

The nine F 27Ms were delivered to the Royal Netherlands Air Force in 1960 and 1961 and now equip No. 334 Squadron, as the primary transport equipment of that service. During 1964, four Troopships were ordered by the Sudanese Air Force.

Span, 95 ft. 2 in.; length, 77 ft. 1½ in.; height, 27 ft. 11 in.; wing area, 754 sq. ft.; aspect ratio, 12; sweepback, nil.

Empty equipped weight, 23,671 lb.; max. payload, 12,029 lb.; max. usable fuel, 9,000 lb. (12,250 lb. with pylon tanks); max. gross weight, 42,000 lb.; max. landing weight, 40,000 lb.

Cruising speed, 295 m.p.h.; initial rate of climb, 1,350 ft./min.; service ceiling, 30,000 ft.; take-off distance to 50 ft., 2,700 ft.; landing distance from 50 ft., 1,940 ft.; typical range, 615 n. miles with 12,029 lb. payload and return with 6,500 lb. payload without refuelling.

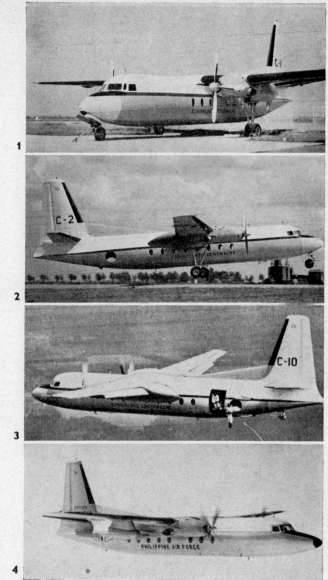

1. *The first F 27 for the R.Neth.A.F., furnished to airline standards.*
2. *A R.Neth.A.F. F 27 at take-off.*
3. *Paratroops drop from an F 27M.*
4. *The F 27 in Philippine Air Force colours.*

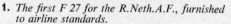

FUJI KM/KM 2 (Japan)

The prototype of the Fuji KM 2 basic trainer for the Japanese Navy.

FOUNDED IN 1953, Fuji Heavy Industries Ltd. is effectively a successor to the well-known pre-War Nakajima Aircraft Company. Immediately upon its formation, the new company concluded a licence and technical assistance agreement with the Beech Aircraft Corporation, in order to produce the Beechcraft T-34 Mentor for the Japanese forces.

Deliveries of the Mentor built by Fuji began in August 1954 and a total of 161 was built—124 for Japan, 36 for the Philippine Air Force and one for the Indonesian Air Force. The Mentor also provided the basis for development of a number of later aircraft by Fuji, as described below.

LM 1 Nikko. This adaptation of the Mentor was produced by Fuji as a four-seat liaison monoplane for the Japanese Ground Self-Defence Force (the Army). First flown on June 6, 1955, the LM 1 used the same wings, landing gear and tail unit as the Mentor, with a new centre fuselage including a four-seat cabin. Power was provided by a 225 h.p. Continental O-470-13. Fuji built 27 LM 1s for service with the Army, in addition to two civil prototypes.

KM. Intended for both civil and military use, the KM was a more powerful version of the LM 1, powered by a 340 h.p. Lycoming GSO-480-B1A6 engine. Navigation equipment and instrumentation were added to permit operation of the KM in all weathers. A prototype was produced by conversion of one of the civil registered LM 1s, and this first flew on December 1, 1958. Delivery of production models to the Japanese Government began in March 1959, the aircraft being earmarked for use in the civil pilot training programme. They are now based at the training school at Ozuki. The prototype KM established a height record in the F.A.I. class L-1C on December 9, 1959 by reaching a height of 32,536 ft.

LM 2. A conversion programme for the LM 1 Nikki began during 1963, introducing a 340 h.p. Lycoming engine and boosting maximum accommodation to five. Some LM 1s in service with the Japanese Ground Self-Defence Force are being converted to LM 2s for use in the liaison rôle.

KM 2. Another derivative of the original Beech Mentor programme, the KM 2 reverts to being a two-seater, but provides side-by-side seating instead of the Beechcraft's tandem seating. Structurally, the KM 2 remains capable of seating four, emphasizing its relationship to the KM Super Nikko, from which it differs only in detail. The first KM 2 was completed in the Spring of 1962 and production orders were placed by the Japanese Maritime Self-Defence Force, which had ordered 40 by the end of 1964. Deliveries began in July 1962.

Power is supplied by a 340 h.p. Lycoming IGSO-480-A1A6 engine. As it uses the original Mentor wing, the KM 2 retains the ability to operate in an armed rôle, particularly for local ground support operations, with underwing bombs or rockets.

The KM 2 is available in utility and aerobatic forms, the latter with a gross weight restriction of 3,330 lb. This restriction on weight gives a small improvement over the performance figures, quoted below, for the standard or utility variant.

Span, 32 ft. 10 in.; length, 26 ft. 0¾ in.; height, 9 ft. 7 in.; wing area, 178 sq. ft.; aspect ratio, 6.1; sweepback, nil.

Empty equipped weight, 2,400 lb.; max. gross weight, 3,860 lb.

Max. speed, 207 m.p.h.; cruising speed, 182 m.p.h.; initial rate of climb, 1,160 ft./min.; service ceiling, 24,000 ft.; take-of distance to 50 ft., 1,855 ft.; landing distance from 50 ft., 1,410 ft.; max. range, 570 miles.

1

2

3

4

1 and **2.** *Views of a Fuji-built T-34 Mentor in flight.*

3. *A Fuji LM-1 Nikko in Japanese Ground Self-Defence Force colours.*

4. *The Fuji KM derivative of the T-34.*

FUJI **T1** (Japan)

A production model of the Fuji T1A.

THE Fuji T1 trainer is Japan's first post-War pure-jet aircraft, and up to 1964 was the only jet type of Japanese design which had been built and flown. Its development began to meet an official Japanese Defence Agency requirement for an aircraft to replace the North American T-6G Texan (Harvard) basic trainer.

The T-6G has been used in Japan as a basic or intermediate trainer, being the second aircraft in the training sequence after *ab initio* construction on the Fuji-built Beech T-34 Mentor. The new aircraft was similarly required for the intermediate rôle and its characteristics consequently are a little more advanced than those of most of the basic jet trainers described in this volume.

To obtain the necessary handling characteristics and performance, Fuji chose a design similar to that of the North American F-86 which was well-known in Japan. With 25 degrees of wing sweep and sweptback tail surfaces, the Fuji T1 has a limiting Mach. No. of 0.85 and duplicates both the low speed and the high speed handling of more advanced types of aircraft.

Tandem seating was selected for the Fuji trainer, it being generally agreed that this gives trainee pilots a more realistic impression of operational conditions than can be obtained with side-by-side seating. The long, one-piece moulded canopy of the T1 hinges up to give access to the cockpit, this being another feature which follows North American practice. Ejection seats are fitted.

Provision is made for one 0.50-in. gun in the fuselage nose, and for various stores on strong points, one under each wing. These can each carry a 100 Imp. gallon drop tank, a machine-gun pod, a Sidewinder air-to-air missile, two air-to-surface missiles, a pack of 7×2.75-in. air-to-air rockets, a 750 lb. bomb or a Napalm bomb.

Following completion of the design, Fuji obtained contracts for prototypes and production orders for two variants. These are as follows:

Fuji T1A. This is the Japanese Air Self-Defence Force designation for the Fuji T1F2. Two prototypes and 40 production models have been built, powered by the 4,000 lb.s.t. Bristol Siddeley Orpheus 805 turbojet. The first prototype flew on January 19, 1958. Delivery of these aircraft began in 1960 and in May 1964 the last T-6 training unit was disbanded, leaving the T1 as the only intermediate trainer in use in the Japanese flying training sequence. The principle school with T1s is at Ashiya.

Fuji T1B. This is the JASDF designation for the Fuji T1F1, which was the initially projected version of the design. It differs from the T1A in having an engine of Japanese design and construction, and it is therefore a wholly indigenous product. The prototype was a converted T1F2, and first flew on May 17, 1960. Subsequently a production batch of 20 was purchased by the JASDF and these were delivered between September 1962 and June 1963. The engine in these aircraft is the 2,645 lb. Ishikawajima-Harima J3-IHI-3. In 1963, Ishikawajima-Harima proposed substitution of the 2,900 lb. J3-IHI-4 engine and production of a further batch of aircraft with this powerplant was being considered.

Data for the T1A follow:
Span, 34 ft. 5 in.; length, 39 ft. 9 in.; height, 13 ft. 4½ in.; wing area, 239 sq. ft.; aspect ratio, 4.96; sweepback, 25 degrees.
Empty weight, 5,335 lb.; gross weight, 11,000 lb. (with external stores).
Max. speed, 575 m.p.h. at 20,000 ft.; cruising speed, 357 m.p.h. at 10,000 ft.; initial rate of climb, 6,500 ft./min.; take-off distance to 50 ft., 2,000 ft.; range, 805 miles (internal tankage) to 1,210 miles (with drop tanks).

1

2

3

4

1. *The Fuji T1F2 (T1A) prototype.*
2 and 3. *Two ground views of the first T1F2.*
4. *A production model T1A with underwing tanks.*

GRUMMAN **E-2 HAWKEYE** (U.S.A.)

A Grumman Hawkeye during carrier acceptance trials.

AT THE END OF a lengthy development period, the Grumman E-2 Hawkeye began to reach units of the U.S. Navy in January 1964 as a replacement for the E-1 Tracer early-warning aircraft. The E-1 (originally WF-2) had been developed from the S-2 (S2F) Tracker to carry long-range search radar which would be able to provide the fleet with early and accurate warning of the approach of potential enemy aircraft or surface vessels. It carried the radar aerials in a large dish-shaped radome over the fuselage—the largest radome designed at that time for a carrier-based aircraft.

The successful development and operation of the Tracer led the U.S. Navy to draw up a specification for a new early warning aircraft. This was the first time that a new aircraft had been specified for this rôle. A design contest was organized, with Grumman selected as the winner and awarded a contract on March 5, 1957. The original designation was W2F-1, changed to E-2 in 1962.

The winning design followed the configuration of the Tracer with a high wing, twin-engined layout and the large radome or "rotodome" above the fuselage. Selected powerplant was two 4,050 h.p. Allison T56-A-8 turboprops driving Aeroproducts 13.5-ft. diameter propellers. The engines are similar to those used in the Lockheed C-130 (see p. 80) but have the output shaft emerging from the top of the reduction gear box so that the air intakes are both below the propeller spinners.

The Hawkeye is designed for carrier operations including catapult take-offs and arrested landings. At high angles of attack, additional lift comes from the "rotodome", so called because it rotates at the rate of six turns per minute. This radome, 24 ft. in diameter, contains stacked antenna elements for the AN/APS-96 search radar.

The first W2F-1 flew on October 21, 1960. Although this was aerodynamically complete, the first aircraft with full electronic equipment did not fly until April 19, 1961. The first automatic interceptions of practice targets were made on February 4, 1963.

As first flown, the Hawkeye had rudders on each of the four vertical tail surfaces. Flight trials showed that this gave too much lateral control power however, and the port inner

surface is now a plain fin. For stowage in below-decks hangars, the wings rotate and fold back, and the rotodome can be lowered 2 ft.

By mid-1963 about 20 E-2As had been built by Grumman and initial carrier trials had been completed. Deliveries to the U.S. Navy began on January 19, 1964, with the first aircraft going to VAW-11 Squadron for training and crew indoctrination.

A COD (carrier on-board delivery) version of the Hawkeye is being delivered by Grumman with the designation C-2A. This aircraft has a completely new pressurized fuselage, minus radome, and incorporating a rear-loading ramp and provision for a 10,000 lb. payload or 39 troops. Two 450 U.S. gallon external fuel tanks can be carried either side of the fuselage, allowing the C-2A to be used as an aerial refuelling tanker or for long ferry flights. Range with full payload is 1,500 miles and the gross weight 54,000 lb. The first of two prototypes of the C-2A flew on November 18, 1964.

Data for the E-2A *follow:*
Span, 80 ft. 7 in.; length, 56 ft. 4 in.; height, 16 ft. 5 in.; wing area, 700 sq. ft.
Empty weight (including 11,000 lb. of electronics) 38,000 lb.; gross weight, 49,500 lb.
Max. speed, 397 m.p.h. at sea level; cruising speed, 220 m.p.h.; initial rate of climb, 4,200 ft./min.; normal operating altitude, 30,000 ft.; endurance, 7 hours.

1

2

3

1. *The prototype W2F-1 Hawkeye.*
2. *A view showing the circular radome and quadruple tail unit.*
3. *The C-2A transport.*

GRUMMAN OV-1 MOHAWK (U.S.A.)

A formation of OV-1As and OV-1Bs (second and fourth aircraft).

DEVELOPMENT OF THE Mohawk, under the Grumman designation of G-134, was initially undertaken to produce an observation aircraft for use both by the U.S. Army and the Marine Corps. The new type was to have STOL capability when operating from rough fields and was to be capable of flying all-weather tactical reconnaissance and support missions for ground forces.

To obtain the required performance, Grumman adopted a twin-engined layout using two Lycoming turboprop engines. The pilot and observer were placed side-by-side in a cockpit which was almost wholly ahead of the airscrew discs for maximum visibility forward and downward. The wing was placed in a shoulder position on the fuselage, leaving ample space below and behind for the wide range of reconnaissance and communications equipment needed.

Grumman won acceptance of the G-134 design in 1957 and the Army and Marine versions were designated AO-1 and OF-1 respectively. Marine interest in the type dwindled, however, and the OF-1 was dropped from the programme before the first flight. The AO-1 was the first aircraft ordered by the U.S. Army to be powered by turboprop engines.

The first contract for the Mohawk, as the type was named, covered a service test batch of nine aircraft designated YAO-IAF. The first of these (57-6463) flew for the first time on April 14, 1959. Production contracts were first placed in 1959 and later contracts have increased the total on order to more than 200. The designation was changed to V-1 in 1961, with the test aircraft then becoming YOV-1A and the production models being as follows:

OV-1A. The basic version of the Mohawk, the principal reconnaissance equipment being the KA-30 camera system. This camera can be rotated from the cockpit to left or right oblique positions and there is space in the nose for a forward camera. For night operations, the OV-1A can carry two pods above the wing roots, each containing 52 upward-firing flares.

OV-1B. This version, first flown in 1960, differs from the OV-1A in having additional equipment for electronic reconnaissance. This equipment comprises the Motorola sideways-looking airborne radar (SLAR) APS-94, carried in a long slender radome beneath the forward fuselage. The APS-94 provides a continuous radar photographic map of the ground on each side of the flight path; this map is recorded on film which can be automatically developed in flight to provide the observer with a print within seconds. Orders for 65 OV-1Bs had been placed by mid-1964.

OV-1C. Third production variant of the Mohawk, the OV-1C is equipped for infra-red reconnaissance, using UAS-4 mapping equipment made by Haller, Raymond and Brown. This equipment is distinguished by a small ventral radome which is not present in the OV-1A or OV-1B. Orders for the OV-1C totalled 24 in mid-1964.

AV-1. The basic OV-1 Mohawk has two underwing pylons carrying 150-U.S. gallon auxiliary tanks. These pylons can be used to carry weapons and two additional pick-ups can be provided under each wing-tip. These six points can carry a total external load of 4,740 lb. of bombs, rockets, machine-gun pods, etc. Armed OV-1 Mohawks have been reported in action in Vietnam. The AV-1 designation would apply to aircraft procured primarily for offensive duties.

Span, 42 ft. 0 in.; length, 41 ft. 0 in.; height, 12 ft. 8 in.; wing area, 330 sq. ft.; aspect ratio, 5.35; sweepback, nil.
Empty equipped weight, 9,028 lb.; gross weight, 11,405 lb.
Max. speed, 324 m.p.h.; cruising speed, 251 m.p.h.; initial climb rate, 2,950 ft./min.; service ceiling, 35,000 ft.; take-off to 50 ft., 475 ft.; landing run from 50 ft., 847 ft.; range (with external tanks), 1,410 miles.

1. *Grumman OV-1A in U.S. Army colours.*
2. *Air-to-air view of the OV-1A.*
3. *An OV-1A with underwing rocket pods.*
4. *An OV-1B in Luftwaffe markings, for evaluation.*

GRUMMAN U-16 ALBATROSS (U.S.A.)

HU-16B in U.S.A.F. Rescue colours.

DEVELOPMENT OF THE Albatross was started by Grumman in 1944 to provide the U.S. Navy with a new general utility aircraft which could be used as an air-sea rescue amphibian, transport, casualty evacuation aircraft and for reconnaissance. Designated XJR2F-1, the prototype flew for the first time on October 24, 1947 and subsequent production totalled more than 450.

In designing the XJR2F-1 (Grumman Model G-64) the makers drew upon more than a decade of experience in producing amphibians for the U.S. Navy and the Albatross design was a successor to the JRF Gray Goose which was widely used during the War. It followed conventional practice for a flying boat amphibian with a deep two-step hull, high wing, fixed stabilizing floats at the wing tips and main wheels retracting into the fuselage sides. It was powered by two 1,425 h.p. R-1820-76 pistons radial engines and provided accommodation for 14 plus a crew of three.

Following successful testing of the prototype, orders for the Albatross were placed by both the U.S. Navy and the U.S.A.F., the latter adopting the new type as standard air-sea rescue equipment and proving, eventually, to be the largest single customer for the type.

The U.S.A.F. designated its new aircraft SA-16As; numerically this was in continuation of the old "OA" category for observation amphibians. The category was changed to "A" for amphibian with "S" used as a prefix for the search version of the Albatross.

When the U.S. Navy ordered the type, the designation was JRSF-1. This changed for a time to PF-1A but designation of the Albatross in the "patrol" category was an evident error and a further change to UF-1A was made when "U" was adopted by the Navy as the new designation for "utility" types in place of "J". The Navy and Coast Guard UF-1s were again re-designated, together with the U.S.A.F. SA-16s, in the unified tri-service scheme of 1962, when they all became members of the U-16 family.

The variants are described below under their current designations but many of these aircraft operated for many years with the earlier designations mentioned above.

HU-16A (SA-16A). The initial production aircraft were for the U.S.A.F. and began to reach M.A.T.S. Air Rescue Service in 1950. These aircraft were equipped specifically for air-sea rescue duties and had accommodation for ten passengers, 12 stretchers or 4,100 lb. of cargo in the hull. A special feature was the "dutch door" in the hull side, the top half of which could be folded down outwards to provide a "counter" for rescue operations. During the Korean conflict alone, SA-16s were credited with saving the lives of more than 900 men.

The U.S.A.F. eventually ordered 305 examples of the SA-16A, including several for supply to other nations under the mutual aid programme. These included Brazil (16), Italy, Nationalist China, the Philippines, Portugal and Spain. Three each have been supplied to the Argentine Air Force and Argentine Navy. All the U.S.A.F. SA-16As were later converted to HU-16B (SA-16B) standard as noted below.

In 1953, triphibian equipment was developed for the Albatross in the form of sprung skis beneath the hull and the wing-tip floats, which did not interfere with land or water operations but allowed the aircraft to land and take-off on snow or ice. After trials the U.S.A.F. ordered 127 conversion kits for this equipment.

HU-16B (SA-16B). Work to improve the performance of the Albatross led to development during 1958 of a new version (the Grumman Model G-111). The principal change was an increase of wing span by 16½ ft., together with a cambered leading edge replacing slots, larger ailerons, better de-icing boots on the leading edges and a taller fin and rudder. The changes improved the speed, range and single-engined climb of the Albatross. A prototype HU-16B flew on January 16, 1956 and all surviving HU-16As entered a programme to be returned to the Grumman plant for modification. The first conversion flew on January 25, 1957.

[Continued on p. 56

1. *The prototype XJR2F-1.*
2. *An early production SA-16A without nose radome.*
3. *U.S. Navy UF-1 in overall blue finish.*
4. *U.S. Coast Guard UF-2G.*

GRUMMAN U-16 ALBATROSS (U.S.A.)

A number of HU-16Bs were supplied to Chile, and special versions were obtained by Canada and Norway. The R.C.A.F. ordered ten for air-sea rescue duties and designated them CSR-110. They were powered by Canadian built Wright R-1820-82 engines, had triphibian landing gear and a new type of retractable landing gear designed to facilitate beaching.

For supply to the Royal Norwegian Air Force under M.D.A.P., the U.S.A.F. initiated development of a special anti-submarine version of the HU-16B. These 16 aircraft have anti-submarine equipment similar to that carried by the S-2 Tracker and including a new large nose radome, magnetic anomaly detector in the tail, underwing searchlight, additional ECM radar, stowage in the hull for sonobuoys, depth charges and marine markers and underwing attachments for torpedoes, rockets or depth charges. Seven similar aircraft were allocated for supply to Spain in 1964.

HU-16C (UF-1). Initial versions of the Albatross delivered to the U.S. Navy were designated UF-1 and were in general similar to the HU-16A. A distinguishing feature of the Navy aircraft was their overall midnight blue finish. Most UF-1s were subsequently modified to HU-16D standard as described below. Eight UF-1s were purchased for use by the Indonesian Air Force and five went into service with the West German Navy.

LU-16C (UF-1L). The U.S. Navy operated a number of UF-1s in the Antarctic for which they were specially winterized, as the "L" suffix of the original designation indicated.

TU-16C (UF-1T). A small number of UF-1s was allocated for use as trainers, with full dual control and provision for training other crew members.

HU-16D (UF-2). The U.S. Navy introduced modifications similar to those of the HU-16B, i.e. long-span wing, cambered leading edge, larger tail surfaces and a general "clean-up" of aerial housings to reduce drag. HU-16Cs were converted to the new standard during routine IRAN (inspect and repair as necessary) programmes. Six aircraft of this type were supplied to the Japanese Maritime Self-Defence Force in 1961.

HU-16E (UF-2G). A number of UF-2s which went into service with the U.S. Coast Guard for air-sea rescue duties around the U.S. coastline now carry this designation. They were originally delivered as UF-1Gs and later converted to UF-2Gs.

Span, 96 ft. 8 in.; length, 61 ft. 3 in.; height, 25 ft. 10 in.; wing area, 1,035 sq. ft.; aspect ratio, 9.0; sweepback, nil.

Empty equipped weight, 22,883 lb.; normal gross weight, 30,353 lb.; max. gross weight, 35,700 lb.

Max. speed, 236 m.p.h.; cruising speed, 150 m.p.h. (124 m.p.h. for max. endurance); initial rate of climb, 1,450 ft./min.; service ceiling, 21,500 ft.; take-off distance to 50 ft., 4,450 ft.; landing distance from 50 ft., 2,200 ft.; max. range, 2,850 miles.

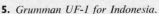

5. *Grumman UF-1 for Indonesia.*
6. *R.C.A.F. Grumman CSR-110.*
7. *Prototype ASW Albatross prior to delivery to Norway.*

GRUMMAN C-4 GULFSTREAM (U.S.A.)

PURCHASE OF TWO Grumman Gulfstreams by the U.S. Coast Guard in 1963 marked the first occasion that the type had been ordered for military duties. Procurement of a further small quantity was planned by the U.S. Navy with 1964 Fiscal Year funds but this prospective order was deleted as an economy measure, for possible re-instatement at a later date.

The Gulfstream originated as a private venture by Grumman for an executive transport powered by two Rolls-Royce Dart turboprops. Its fuselage size was strictly limited to the optimum for executive users as shown by extensive Grumman studies and the maximum number of seats in a high density layout is no more than 24. Most of the more-than-100 Gulfstreams built to date are furnished to seat only 10–12 passengers.

An auxiliary power unit is carried to make the Gulfstream independent of outside power supply for engine starting, cabin conditioning and operation of the built-in, hydraulically-operated airsteps at the forward door.

The first Gulfstream flew on August 14, 1958. Two examples were purchased by the U.S. Coast Guard off the shelf in 1963 for service as V.I.P. transports and these were designated VC-4As. The projected version for the U.S. Navy was the TC-4B which would be equipped for the dual rôles of navigation trainer and transport. One executive Gulfstream has been delivered to the Greek Air Force.

Span, 67 ft. 6 in.; length, 63 ft. 9 in.; height, 22 ft. 9 in.; wing area, 610 sq. ft.; aspect ratio, 10; sweepback, nil.

Empty equipped weight, 21,900 lb.; payload, 4,270 lb.; gross weight, 35,100 lb.; max. landing weight, 33,600 lb.; max. zero fuel weight, 26,170 lb.

Max. cruising speed, 348 m.p.h. at 25,000 ft.; normal cruising speed, 288 m.p.h. at 25,000 ft.; initial rate of climb, 1,900 ft./min.; service ceiling, 36,000 ft.; take-off balanced field length, 4,370 ft.; landing field length required, 2,680 ft.; range, 2,540 miles with max. fuel and 2,740 lb. payload.

1 *and* **2.** *Pre-delivery pictures of the Grumman VC-4A for the U.S. Coast Guard.*

HANDLEY PAGE **HERALD** (Great Britain)

Handley Page Herald Series 400, Royal Malaysian Air Force.

MILITARY VERSIONS of the Handley Page Herald are based on the Herald airliner, conceived more than a decade ago. Designed at the company's Reading factory, the original HPR-3 was a 44-seat feeder liner, powered by four Alvis Leonides Major piston engines.

Two prototypes of this aircraft were built, as a company-funded venture, with the first flight of G-AODE being made at Woodley Aerodrome on August 25, 1955. The second prototype, G-AODF, followed a year later. With provisional export orders for some 30 aircraft, Handley Page established a production line of Heralds but by the end of 1956 interest in a piston-engined aircraft of this class was waning rapidly.

Under the designation HPR-7, therefore, the Herald was re-designed to be powered by two Rolls-Royce Dart R.Da.7 turboprops. Apart from a new centre-section with the new nacelles, few changes were needed but the fuselage was lengthened by 20 in. The two prototypes were converted to the new form and first flew, respectively, on August 30 and December 17, 1958.

Production models to the same standard as these prototypes began to appear in 1959, the first (G-APWA) flying on October 30 in that year. Only four aircraft were in fact built in this initial version, the Series 100, including three for B.E.A. Subsequent production aircraft have a 3 ft. 6 in. fuselage extension and higher operating weights. These are the Series 200, the first of which was the prototype G-AODF converted and flown on April 8, 1961.

The first military customer for the Herald was the Royal Arab Air Force (Jordan) which ordered two Series 200s, furnished as staff transports. After little more than a year in service, these two aircraft were transferred to the Jordan airline Alia.

In 1962, the Royal Malaysian Air Force selected the Herald to meet its needs for a tactical troop transport capable of moving comparatively large numbers of troops and supplies over fairly long distances. The type adopted for Malaysian operations was the Series 400, a militarized Series 200, and the R.M.A.F. order totalled eight.

Special features of the Herald 400 series include a reinforced floor, and reinforced fuselage door surround, to permit the air-drop of supplies and paratroops. The R.M.A.F. Heralds can carry 50 troops (in rearward-facing seats) or 24 stretchers with attendants. Roller track can be attached to the floor and used, with a ball transfer mat adjacent to the rear loading door, to handle pallets (a maximum of eight 1,500 lb. pallets can be carried).

The double loading doors in the Herald are large enough to permit the loading and un-loading of small wheeled or tracked vehicles—for example three Austin "Mokes" or three mortars and two half-ton trailers. One portion of the double door can be opened in the air for paratroop dropping; both portions slide away inside the fuselage for air-dropping of supplies.

Prior to delivery of the first Herald Series 400, the first production Series 100, G-APWA, was leased to the Tentera Udara Diraja Malaysia (R.M.A.F.) for several weeks operation from Kuala Lumpar. The first four Series 400s were delivered without the modification permitting air-opening of the fuselage door.

Span, 94 ft. 9 in.; length, 75 ft. 6 in.; height, 24 ft.; wing area, 586 sq. ft.; aspect ratio, 10.2; sweepback, nil.
Empty equipped weight, 25,286 lb.; max. internal payload, 11,714 lb.; max. gross weight, 43,000 lb.; max. landing weight, 39,500 lb.; max. zero fuel weight, 37,000 lb.
Max. cruising speed, 265 knots; cruising speed, 215 knots; initial rate of climb, 1,805 ft./min.; service ceiling, 27,900 ft.; take-off distance to 50 ft., 3,960 ft.; landing distance from 50 ft., 2,140 ft.; range with max. fuel, 1,350 miles; range with max. payload, 910 miles; ferry range, 2,250 miles.

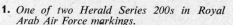

1. *One of two Herald Series 200s in Royal Arab Air Force markings.*
2. *An R.M.A.F. Herald Series 400.*
3. *Supply-drop by an R.M.A.F. Herald.*
4. *A Herald Series 400 at take-off.*

1

2

3

4

HAWKER SIDDELEY 748 ANDOVER (Great Britain)

Prototype Hawker Siddeley Andover, G-ARRV, with rear doors open.

VERSIONS OF THE Hawker Siddeley 748 for military use fall into two categories. The first comprises executive and personnel transports which are similar in most respects to the airline version of the 748; the second type is the 748 MF, a tactical transport with rear loading and other special features.

The design dates back to 1957 when the Avro company embarked upon development of a small turboprop-engined feeder-liner for civil use. This was put into production as a private venture in January 1959 and before the end of that year an agreement was concluded with the Indian Government permitting the manufacture of a version of the 748 in India for use by the Air Force there.

With Avro assistance, the Indian Air Force established a production line for the 748 at the I.A.F. Maintenance Base at Kanpur (this is now known as the I.A.F. Aircraft Manufacturing Depot). Avro supplied components for the construction of four Series 1 748s (Dart 514 engines) and the first of these to be assembled at Kanpur made its first flight on November 1, 1961; the first Series 2 aircraft (Dart 531 engines) first flew on January 28, 1964.

Aircraft of the Series 2 type have also been purchased for military service from Hawker Siddeley. Six ordered by the Brazilian Air Force are now in service with the Special Transport Group and six others ordered by the Royal Air Force were being delivered in 1964. These are identified as Andover CC.Mk.2, as noted below.

Andover C.Mk.1. Special military versions of the 748 were under study in the Avro design office as early as 1959 and a wide range of possibilities was investigated, including high- and low-wing variants and versions with side and rear loading.

To provide the rear-loading capability, a completely new rear fuselage was designed for the 748 MF, as the tactical transport became known. This incorporates clam-shell type doors covering the rear of the opening, plus a lower door section which hinges down to form part of the loading ramp. A unique "kneeling" landing gear has been developed for the 748, which permits the main landing gear units to be partially retracted with the aircraft on the ground, giving a range of movement at the rear door sill between 7 ft. 2 in. and 3 ft. 3 in.

The 748 MF was selected by the R.A.F. in 1962 and a production contract for 31 was placed. While production was being initiated, the prototype Avro 748 was modified to have the new rear fuselage and 3,000 s.h.p. Dart R.Da.12 engines and flew in this new form on December 21, 1963. Originally G-APZV, it was re-registered G-ARRV as the prototype 748 MF. Production aircraft for the R.A.F. have been named Andover C.Mk.1. and have Dart 201 engines.

Andover CC.Mk.2. Six examples of the Hawker Siddeley 748 Series 2 were ordered in 1963 with this designation. Two have been allocated to the Queen's Flight and the first of these flew on May 15, 1964. It was handed over on July 9, 1964. The other four are furnished as V.I.P. and staff transports for use by R.A.F. Transport Command.

Data for the Andover C.Mk.1:
Span, 98 ft. 0 in.; length, 77 ft. 11 in.; height, 29 ft. 5 in.; wing area, 831 sq. ft.; aspect ratio, 11.967; sweepback, nil.
Empty equipped weight, 27,700 lb.; max. payload, 15,723 lb.; gross weight, 50,000 lb.; max. landing weight, 47,600 lb.
Cruising speed, 270 m.p.h.; take-off distance to 50 ft., 1,980 ft.; landing distance from 50 ft., 1,520 ft.; range with max. payload, 500 miles; range with 4,000 lb. payload, 2,100 miles.

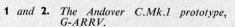

1 *and* 2. *The Andover C.Mk.1 prototype, G-ARRV.*
3. *An H.S. 748 Srs.2 of the Brazilian Air Force.*
4. *A Queen's Flight Andover CC.Mk.2.*
5. *First Indian-assembled H.S. 748.*

HAWKER SIDDELEY 660 ARGOSY C.Mk.1 (Great Britain)

Two Hawker Siddeley Argosies of R.A.F. Transport Command.

THE FORMER Armstrong Whitworth company, now absorbed in the Avro Whitworth Division of Hawker Siddeley, embarked upon the design of a tactical transport in the early 'fifties to meet an official requirement for a Valetta replacement. The project studies were designated AW66 and were for a twin-engined aeroplane having a twin boom layout with a capacious fuselage and "straight-in" front and rear loading.

The AW66 and a competitive (and generally similar) design by Short Bros. and Harland were thoroughly evaluated by the Air Ministry but neither was ordered even in prototype form. Against this background of official indecision, the Hawker Siddeley Group decided, in 1956, to lay down a batch of ten aircraft based on the AW66 design but intended for commercial use.

This private venture aircraft was designated the AW650, the type number AW65 having previously been reserved for civil versions of the AW66. The layout of the AW650, later named Argosy, was similar to that of the military project, and four Rolls-Royce Darts in Viscount 800-type nacelles were adopted as the powerplant. To save both time and development costs, the wing was derived from that of the Avro Shackleton, its design being completed in the Avro drawing office as Type 733.

The first of the civil Argosy freighters made its first flight on January 8, 1959, and all ten were subsequently sold for airline operation. An official decision to adopt the type for use by the R.A.F. followed and a series of contracts brought the total orders for the Argosy C.Mk.1 to 56.

In adapting the design to meet R.A.F. requirements, several significant changes were made to allow the Argosy C.Mk.1 to operate at higher weights—up to 105,000 lb. compared with the AW650's 88,000 lb. This involved changes in the wing structure and to the landing gear, and required the use of more powerful engines—2,680 e.s.h.p. Dart R.Da.8 Mk.101s with water-methanol injection.

To accommodate weather radar the fuselage nose doors were deleted, and a flight-refuelling probe was added above the flight deck roof.

Another major requirement was that the rear loading doors should be air-openable for supply dropping and the original side-hinged door was replaced by a "beaver tail" type. An aerodynamic mock-up of this new rear door arrangement was fitted temporarily to one of the civil machines, G-APRL, in which form it first flew on July 28, 1960.

The first Argosy C.Mk.1 (XN814) flew on March 4, 1961 and deliveries began at the end of the same year. Squadrons equipped include Nos. 114 and 267. Delivery of all 56 aircraft for the R.A.F. was completed in April 1964.

The military Argosy is operated by a flight crew of four and provides accommodation for 69 equipped troops or 48 stretchers plus four attendants. Palletized freight can be loaded by means of the R.A.F. standard roller conveyor system in the floor, and the equipment which can be accommodated includes the Saracen armoured car, 105 mm. howitzer, Ferret scout car and Wombat anti-tank gun. As a paratrooper the Argosy carries 54 troops and has paratroop doors for simultaneous use on each side of the rear fuselage.

The Argosy can be refuelled in flight by Valiant and Victor tankers using the probe-and-drogue method, at all weights up to the maximum overload of 105,000 lb. One Argosy has also been used for development of the Smith's Mk.10C military auto-landing system.

Span, 115 ft. 0 in.; length, 89 ft. 0 in.; height, 27 ft. 0 in.; wing area, 1,458 sq. ft.; aspect ratio, 9.07; sweepback, nil.
Empty equipped weight, 57,400 lb.; max. payload, 29,000 lb.; normal gross weight, 97,000 lb.; max. overload weight, 105,000 lb.
Cruising speed, 269 m.p.h. at 20,000 ft. and 80,000 lb.; performance ceiling, 18,500 ft.; landing distance from 50 ft., 3,500 ft.; range with max. payload, 345 miles; range with max. fuel, 1,070 miles; max. ferry range, 3,250 miles.

1. *An Argosy C.Mk.1 with rear doors open.*
2. *Paratroops dropping from an Argosy.*
3. *An Argosy with refuelling probe in action.*
4. *Ground view of an R.A.F. Argosy.*

HAWKER SIDDELEY **COMET** (Great Britain)

A Comet C.Mk.4C of R.A.F. Transport Command.

IN COMMON WITH almost every other type of aircraft operated by R.A.F.'s Transport Command since the end of World War II, the military Comet is derived from a commercial transport version. Its adoption by the R.A.F. initially sprang from the cancellation of plans to operate the Comet 2 commercially after a series of disasters to the Comet 1.

The first Comet prototype (G-ALVG) flew on July 27, 1949 and the second on the same date one year later. These aircraft, like the production Comet 1s, were powered by four de Havilland Ghost turbojets. Scheduled operations with Comet 1s began on May 2, 1952 but were withdrawn in April 1954 after a series of accidents which were eventually attributed to fatigue failures of the pressure cabin structure.

At the time the Comet was grounded, a new version was in production, as the Comet 2, with a slightly longer fuselage and powered by Rolls-Royce Avon engines. The first Comet 2 (G-AMXA) flew on August 27, 1953, and 22 aircraft were in various stages of flight test or production when the Comet 1 was grounded. After the accident investigation had been completed, 13 of these 22 aircraft were transferred to the R.A.F., including ten for Transport Command.

The first two Comets for Transport Command were designated T.Mk.2s and were equipped for use as crew trainers as well as personnel transports. They had been completed as G-AMXB and G-AMXF and became XK669 and XK670 respectively, the first flight of a T.Mk.2 being made on December 9, 1955. Eight more aircraft were completed as C.Mk.2s from the Comet 2 components already in production.

These ten Comets, which went into service with No. 216 Squadron, R.A.F., were structurally modified to prevent recurrence of the fatigue failures, and were "lifed" at 8,000 hours. They also had a new cargo floor installed, provision for up to 48 rearward-facing seats and increased gross weight of 120,000 lb.

Three other Comet 2s already flying at the time of the grounding in 1954 were allocated to No. 90 Group (later Signals Command) for special duties in the development of radar and electronics while another, after being used as a

Series 2E for Avon engine development, went to the R.A.E. for radio and navaid trials.

While the Comet C.2s were operating around the World with the R.A.F., commercial development produced the Comet 4, 4B and 4C, with a lengthened fuselage and many detail changes. The R.A.F. purchased five Comet 4Cs from the final production batch of the type, and these went into service, also with No. 216 Squadron, in 1962.

The first Comet C.Mk.4C, as this version is officially designated, flew for the first time on November 15, 1961. In accordance with R.A.F. policy, it has rearward-facing seats for a normal load of 86 passengers or a maximum of 94. In all respects other than cabin and flight deck details, the C.Mk.4C is similar to the commercial Comet 4C, data for which are given below.

One other Comet 4C operating in military markings was purchased by the Ministry of Aviation in 1963 for long-range navaid development.

Span, 114 ft. 10 in.; length, 118 ft. 0 in.; height, 29 ft. 6 in.; wing area, 2,121 sq. ft.; sweep-back, 20 degrees.
Empty equipped weight, 79,600 lb.; gross weight, 162,000 lb.
Cruising speed, 542 m.p.h. at 31,000 ft.; take-off field length, 6,750 ft.; landing distance from 30 ft., 5,740 ft. (using engine reverse thrust); range, 2,590 miles with 19,630 lb. payload.

1

2

3

1 *and* 2. *Views of a Comet C.Mk.2 of No. 216 Squadron, R.A.F.*
3. *A Comet C.Mk.4C at take-off.*

HAWKER SIDDELEY **GNAT** (Great Britain)

Hawker Siddeley Gnat trainers in R.A.F. service.

THE MOST ADVANCED trainer produced to date in Britain, the Gnat T.Mk.1 trainer provides the second stage in the Royal Air Force all-through jet training scheme. It entered service at the end of 1962 with Flying Training Schools as a replacement for the de Havilland Vampire T.Mk.11, and is used in conjunction with the Hunting Jet Provost *ab initio* trainer.

Based on the single-seat Gnat fighter, the trainer has a number of important modifications. Increased fuselage length permits the installation of a second seat, in tandem with the first; both are Folland-developed 4GT ejection seats for use from runway level upwards at speeds above 90 knots. A larger wing has been introduced, giving 40 per cent more area to reduce the landing speed, but with a lower thickness/chord ratio (7 per cent instead of 8 per cent) to maintain the high-speed performance.

Equipment in the trainer was extensively re-designed and modified, in particular to provide the OR946 flight instrumentation as used in the Lightning and other operational types. The standardized layout of OR946 made it necessary to re-design much of the Gnat cockpit and a new windscreen, minus gunsight and bullet-proof frame, was fitted.

Power in the trainer, as in the fighter Gnats, is supplied by a single Bristol Siddeley Orpheus turbojet. For economy, the engine is derated from its full military thrust of 4,720 lb. to 4,400 lb. in the Orpheus 101 which powers the Gnat T.Mk.1.

In R.A.F. service, the Gnat trainer is used only for pilot training, and underwing stores normally comprise nothing but two 59 gal. fuel tanks, flush fitting at the leading edge. A wide range of underwing stores can be carried by the Gnat, however, to suit it to weapons training. Possible loads include two 500 lb. bombs; two Aden gun pods; two rocket pods; or two Bullpup or Sidewinder missiles. Reconnaissance camera pods or additional fuel tanks can also be carried beneath the wings.

A contract for a development batch of 14 Gnat T.Mk.1s was placed with Folland in March 1958 and the first aircraft (XM691) flew for the first time on August 31, 1959. The initial aircraft in this batch were used for various aspects of the development programme, related particularly to the new features of the Gnat trainer. Thus the third aircraft, XM693, was the first to incorporate full dual control; XM694 was the first with the production standard integral fuel tanks in the wings and XM698 was the first with the OR946 integrated instrument display, plus a slightly lengthened nose ahead of the cockpit. The last-mentioned Gnat XM698 was also fitted with a full-rated Orpheus 701 (4,700 lb.s.t.) for comparative trials.

The first production contract for Gnat trainers was placed in July 1960, for 30 aircraft; two later contracts for 20 and 41 brought the total on order by March 1962 to 105. Deliveries of production Gnats began in November 1962, to No. 4 F.T.S. at Valley and to the C.F.S. at Little Rissington. The R.A.F. training syllabus provides for 70 hours flying on the Gnat before pilots graduate to an O.C.U.; time to solo is about 6 hours for pupils having previously flown 160 hours on the Jet Provost.

Span, 24 ft. 0 in.; length, 31 ft. 9 in.; height, 10 ft. 0 in.; wing area, 175 sq. ft.; aspect ratio, 3.29; sweepback, 40 degrees.
Empty equipped weight, 5,639 lb.; gross weight (clean), 8,039 lb.; gross weight (with external tanks), 9,107 lb.
Max. level speed, M=0.95 (628 m.p.h. at 36,100 ft.); max. speed in dive, M=1.15; initial rate of climb, 7,620 ft./min.; service ceiling, 48,000 ft.; take-off distance to 50 ft., 2,550 ft.; landing distance from 50 ft., 3,000 ft. (2,210 ft. with braking parachute); max. range (with external fuel), 1,180 miles.

1

2

3

1. *The first development Gnat T.Mk.1, XM691.*
2. *A production Gnat T.Mk.1 from No. 4 F.T.S.*
3. *The development Gnat XM693, used for engine trials.*
4. *A Gnat T.Mk.1 at the Central Flying School.*

4

HAWKER SIDDELEY 125 DOMINIE (Great Britain)

1

2

3

PURCHASED BY THE R.A.F. as a replacement for the Varsity navigation trainer, the Hawker Siddeley 125 was designed initially as a small executive jet aircraft. Its detail design began in April 1961 in the de Havilland drawing office, after considerable research into the possible market for this type of aircraft.

Layout of the 125 was along "baby airliner" lines, with rear-mounted engines and a high tail, as used in the H.S.121 Trident. To meet the requirement for a 3,000 lb. thrust engine to power the 125, Bristol Siddeley developed a new version of the Viper. This ASV.20 variant has an additional compressor stage and higher operating temperatures than had been used previously and has given rise to a new family of Vipers with higher ratings. Production models of the H.S.125 have 3,120 lb.s.t. Viper 521 (civil) or Viper 301 (military) engines.

The first H.S.125 (G-ARYA) flew for the first time on August 13, 1962, followed by the second (G-ARYB) on December 12, 1962. These aircraft were essentially prototypes and were built at the main de Havilland works at Hatfield; the main production line is at Chester, and the first production aircraft (G-ARYC) flew on February 12, 1963.

In addition to small changes between the prototypes and production aircraft, the fuselage length was increased by 1 ft. and the main entrance door was widened. Deliveries of the executive H.S.125 began in 1964 following certification on September 28.

A range of military variants of the H.S.125 has been projected. One of these variants, the navigational trainer, was adopted by the R.A.F. in September 1962 when an order was placed for 20 examples. Subsequently the name Dominie T.Mk.1 was chosen for this type. The layout provides for three students and an instructor in the rear cabin, the forward part being taken up by equipment racks. Air search radar is fitted in the nose. The first Dominie made its first flight on December 1, 1964.

Other military versions of the H.S.125 include a communications aircraft with 12 seats and a variant for casualty evacuation with six stretchers and two seats. Also projected is a NASARR trainer, with a lengthened nose containing the scanner.

Span, 47 ft. 0 in.; length, 47 ft. 5 in.; height, 16 ft. 6 in.; wing area, 353 sq. ft.; aspect ratio, 6.25; sweepback, 20 degrees.
Empty equipped weight, 11,000 lb.; gross weight, 20,800 lb.
Max. speed, 500 m.p.h. at 25,000 ft.; cruising speed, 420 m.p.h.; initial rate of climb, 4,000 ft./min.; service ceiling, 25,000 ft.; take-off distance to 35 ft., 3,580 ft.; landing distance from 50 ft., 2,270 ft.; range, 1,600 miles with max. fuel, 1,400 miles with max. load.

1. *Prototype H.S.125, G-ARYA.*
2. *The third H.S.125, with lengthened fuselage, used for engine development.*
3. *The first production Dominie T.Mk.1, XS709.*

HELIO U-10 (U.S.A.)

THE SHORT TAKE-OFF and landing characteristics of the Helio Courier make it particularly suitable for military operations in the counter-insurgency rôle, and it is for this purpose that the largest quantity has been purchased for use by the U.S.A.F.

A single example of the original H 391 Courier was evaluated by the U.S. Army as the YL-24. Subsequently, in 1958, three examples of the more powerful H 395 Super Courier were purchased for evaluation by the U.S. Air Force. They were designated L-28A and were subjected to a number of trials, including a series of flights from Warren A.F.B. to evaluate the L-28A for transportation purposes and, more particularly, missile site support. These trials established that the L-28A was simple to operate and that pilot conversion to the type could be accomplished "very rapidly and efficiently".

In 1961 the L-28A was re-designated U-10A and in 1962 quantity procurement by the U.S.A.F. began, primarily for use in Vietnam in the counter-insurgency rôle. This involved, in particular, flying behind the enemy lines with supplies and/or personnel, when the aircraft's ability to land in small fields was of particular advantage. To meet the urgent requirements of the U.S.A.F., Helio purchased a number of Couriers from their civilian owners and refurbished them for military use, in addition to building new aircraft. A further contract in July 1963 called for 44 U-10s, of which 24 were for the Air National Guard Air Commando Group and 20 were for the Army.

In addition to the U-10A, Helio has developed

the U-10B, with a 60 U.S. gallon fuel tank in the wing to bring the total capacity to 120 gallons—sufficient to give the aircraft a range of some 1,700 miles and an endurance of well over 10 hours. Also reported is a U-10C version with a 360 h.p. Lycoming GSO-540 engine and provision for supplies or weapon packs to be carried beneath the wings. Standard powerplant for the U-10A and U-10B is the 295 h.p. GO-480 engine.

Span, 39 ft. 0 in.; length, 30 ft. 0 in.; height, 8 ft. 10 in.; wing area, 231 sq. ft.; aspect ratio, 6.58; sweepback, nil.
Empty weight, 2,037 lb.; gross weight, 3,920 lb. (U-10C, 4,000 lb.).
Max. speed, 176 m.p.h. at sea level; cruising speed, 150 m.p.h. at 10,000 ft.; initial rate of climb, 1,350 ft./min.; service ceiling, 22,500 ft.; take-off distance to 50 ft., 475 ft.; landing distance from 50 ft., 355 ft.; normal range, 800 miles.

1. *A Helio Courier being demonstrated outside the Pentagon.*
2 *and* **3**. *Two views of a U.S.A.F. L-28A, forerunner of the U-10.*

HINDUSTAN **HAOP-27 KRISHAK** (India)

WORK ON A LIGHT two-seat aircraft of conventional high-wing layout was started by Hindustan Aircraft Ltd. at Bangalore, India, during 1958, with the object of producing a general purpose aircraft for club or military use. The result, called the Pushpak, flew for the first time on September 28, 1958 and a production batch of 70 was put in hand.

In parallel with development of the Pushpak, HAL began work on a larger version called the Krishak, powered by a 190 h.p. Continental engine. The prototype (BR459) first flew in November 1959 and the second Krishak (BR460, illustrated) followed a year later.

The Krishak normally carries a pilot and two or three passengers. For operation in the AOP rôle, the Krishak was ordered into production in 1963 with a contract for 30 for the Indian Army, designated HAOP-27.

Data for the Krishak have not been released. The following specifications refer to the Pushpak:

Span, 36 ft. 0 in.; length, 21 ft. 0 in.; height, 9 ft. 1 in.; wing area, 175 sq. ft.
Empty weight, 870 lb.; max. gross weight, 1,350 lb.
Max. speed, 90 m.p.h. at sea level; initial rate of climb, 500 ft./min.; service ceiling, 14,000 ft.; range, 250 miles.

HINDUSTAN **HT-2** (India)

HINDUSTAN AIRCRAFT LTD produced its first aircraft of original design in 1951. This was the HT-2 basic trainer, which was still in small-scale production in 1964. The Hindustan company, at Bangalore, had previously built several types of foreign design under licence and had been responsible in India for the maintenance and servicing of Douglas DC-3s and other types.

The HT-2 is a conventional low-wing monoplane of all-metal construction, with the two seats in tandem beneath a long cockpit canopy. The prototype first flew on August 13 1957 and was powered by a de Havilland Gipsy Major 10 engine; a second prototype, flown on February 19, 1952, had the more powerful 155 h.p. Blackburn Cirrus Major III engine which is used in production models also.

Production deliveries to the Indian Air Force began in 1953 and the majority of the 160 or so built have gone to this service, to the Indian Navy and to the Indian Civil Aviation Training Centre. Twelve were sold to the Ghana Air Force.

Span, 35 ft. 2 in.; length, 24 ft. 8½ in.; height, 8 ft. 11 in.; wing area, 173.4 sq. ft.; aspect ratio, 7.13; sweepback, nil.
Empty weight, 1,540 lb.; gross weight, 2,240 lb.
Max. speed, 130 m.p.h.; cruising speed, 105 m.p.h.; initial rate of climb, 800 ft./min.; service ceiling, 14,500 ft.; max. range, 350 miles.

1. *The second prototype Krishak.*
2. *An HT-2 supplied to the Royal Singapore Flying Club.*
3. *HT-2s in Indian Air Force markings.*

HUNTING JET PROVOST (Great Britain)

PRE-PRODUCTION MODELS of the Jet Provost were used for the first basic pilot training course ever conducted on jet aircraft by the Royal Air Force. This course was started in September 1955 at No. 2 Flying Training School, R.A.F. Hullavington, and represented an important milestone in the history of pilot training in Britain.

The 18 students, arbitrarily chosen, who formed the first course, and who subsequently went on to complete their training on the Vampire T.Mk.11, were the first in the R.A.F. to be trained exclusively on jet aircraft. The success of this course and a second one at Hullavington led to production orders for the Jet Provost and its selection as the basic jet trainer for the R.A.F.

Development of the P.84 Jet Provost had begun as early as 1950 as a private venture by Hunting Percival Aircraft (the company subsequently became Hunting Aircraft Ltd. and was absorbed by British Aircraft Corporation to become the B.A.C. (Luton) division in 1964). As the name suggested, it was a straightforward development of the piston-engined P.56 Provost. The latter had been built to an official specification for a new basic trainer to replace the immediately post-War Prentice.

Before the end of 1951, the Air Ministry indicated its interest in the jet development of the Provost and the design moved into the detail stage. The aim was to produce a basic jet trainer as cheaply and quickly as possible to permit evaluation of the jet aircraft.

Changes in the design were mostly concerned with the installation of an Armstrong Siddeley Viper ASV.5 turbojet in place of the Alvis Leonides piston engine. This meant lengthening the fuselage and moving the cockpit relatively further forward to compensate for the weight of the engine in the rear fuselage.

Air intakes of D-section were added each side of the fuselage, ahead of the wing roots. Some re-design of the wing structure was needed to increase the fuel capacity and to provide for retraction of the undercarriage. The wing profile was altered at the roots to maintain the low-speed handling qualities despite the absence of propeller slipstream, and spoiler/air brakes were added above and below the wing.

Extra side area was needed at the tail to compensate for the forward shift of the cockpit, and provision was made for wing-tip tanks to be fitted.

In March 1953, Hunting received a contract covering construction of a pre-production batch of Jet Provosts. These appeared as T.Mk.1s and are described below together with other variants which have since appeared.

Jet Provost T.Mk.1. Ten aircraft with this designation were ordered for service trials but the tenth was completed as a T.Mk.2 (see below). The Mk.1s were numbered XD674–XD680 and XD692–XD693 inclusive. In addition, Hunting built a company-owned demonstrator G-AOBU. The first Jet Provost, XD674, flew on June 26, 1954 and was powered by a 1,640 lb.s.t. Viper 101 engine. In addition to the changes described above, it flew initially with an additional dorsal fin. This later gave way to a small ventral fin. Seven of the nine Service T.Mk.1s went to No. 2 F.T.S., R.A.F. Hullavington, for experimental jet basic training courses which began in September 1955. The other two remained in use as development airframes. The demonstrator G-AOBU flew for a time with external tanks under the wing tips and was later used by Armstrong Siddeley as G-42-1 for flight development of the Viper ASV.8.

Jet Provost T.Mk.2. The last of the ten pre-production aircraft ordered in 1953, XD694, was completed to a new standard with several important modifications, and first flew on September 1, 1955. The changes included replacing the pneumatic system by a hydraulic one for undercarriage, flaps, air brakes and wheel brakes; shortening the undercarriage by approximately 3 ft. and re-designing the rear fuselage for better airflow and to accommodate

[Continued on p. 73

1

2

3

4

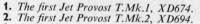

1. *The first Jet Provost T.Mk.1, XD674.*
2. *The first Jet Provost T.Mk.2, XD694.*
3. *A T.Mk.2 trials aircraft, G-AOUS.*
4. *The T.Mk.2 demonstrator G-AOHD.*

HUNTING JET PROVOST (Great Britain)

A Hunting Jet Provost T.Mk.52 in the colours of the Venezuelan Air Force.

the larger tailpipe of the 1,750 lb.s.t. Viper 102 (ASV.8) engine. The fuselage re-design included use of a dorsal fin replacing the ventral fin of the Mk.1, and the wing-tip tanks were re-designed to be mounted on the centre line instead of beneath the tip.

In addition to XD694, Hunting built three development Mk.2s as a private venture jointly with Armstrong Siddeley Motors. The first of these, registered G-AOHD, was later evaluated by the R.A.A.F. as A99-001; the others were G-23-1 and G-AOUS. During 1957, G-23-1 was fitted with a one-piece moulded windscreen, a single central flight instrument panel and Martin Baker ejection seats—all features of the subsequent production models. G-AOUS was used for armament development, with two 0.303 in. machine-guns in the engine intake walls and underwing points for 12 rockets, or 8 practice bombs. During trials at the A. and A.E.E., Boscombe Down, it was numbered XN117, subsequently reverting to G-AOUS and being fitted with a 2,500 lb.s.t. Viper 201 (ASV.11) for trials leading to development of the Jet Provost T.Mk.4.

Jet Provost T.Mk.3. First flown on June 22, 1958, the T.Mk.3 was the production version ordered by the R.A.F. early in 1957 as its new standard basic trainer. Powered by a Viper 102, this variant was similar to the T.Mk.2 described above with the addition of detail improvements and equipment as specified by the R.A.F. The first aircraft was XM346 and deliveries began on June 26, 1959.

Jet Provost T.Mk.4. As noted above, the Mk.2 development aircraft G-AOUS was fitted with a 2,500 lb.s.t. Viper 201 engine, providing a significant improvement in performance. The increase in power in no way detracted from the advantages of the Jet Provost as a basic trainer, but increased the versatility of the aircraft and allowed students to reach a more advanced stage of flying on it. The R.A.F. ordered two Mk.3s to be completed with the new engine for evaluation and after trials with these two aircraft (XM467 and XM468) orders were placed for this variant as the T.Mk.4.

Jet Provost T.Mk.5. Initially developed as the BAC 145, this version of the Jet Provost intro-

duces a pressurized cockpit and increased fuel capacity. Gross weight is 9,200 lb. A contract was placed in 1964 for a prototype conversion from a Jet Provost 4.

Jet Provost T.Mk.51. Export version of the T.Mk.3 with Viper 102 engine plus full provision for armament as described under T.Mk.2 above. Orders include 12 for Royal Ceylon Air Force, four for Sudan Air Force and six for Kuwait Air Force.

Jet Provost T.Mk.52. Export version of the T.Mk.4 with Viper 201 and full armament provision. Ordered by Sudan Air Force (4), Venezuelan Air Force (15) and Iraqi Air Force (20).

BAC 164. Projected counter-insurgency version of the Jet Provost 4 with six wing strongpoints for a total external load of 3,100 lb. Powered by a 3,410 lb. Viper 522 (ASV.20). Gross weight 10,500 lb. (operational) or 11,500 lb. (ferry).

BAC 166. Trial installation of Viper 522 in the final production Jet Provost T.Mk.4, XS231. First flown on March 16, 1965.

BAC 167. As BAC 164, with pressure cabin as Jet Provost 5. Optional armour protection and self-sealing fuel tanks.

Data for the Jet Provost T.Mk.4:
Span, 36 ft. 11 in.; length, 32 ft. 5 in.; height, 10 ft. 2 in.; wing area, 213.7 sq. ft.; aspect ratio, 5.84; sweepback, nil.
Empty equipped weight, 4,650 lb.; gross weight, 7,400 lb.
Max. speed, 410 m.p.h. at 20,000 ft.; initial rate of climb, 3,400 ft./min.; take-off distance to 50 ft., 2,200 ft.; landing dsitance from 50 ft., 2,050 ft.; range, 700 miles at 30,000 ft. on max. fuel.

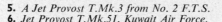

5. *A Jet Provost T.Mk.3 from No. 2 F.T.S.*
6. *Jet Provost T.Mk.51, Kuwait Air Force.*
7. *Jet Provost T.Mk.51, Ceylon Air Force.*
8. *Jet Provost T.Mk.52, Iraqi Air Force.*

5

6

7

8

HISPANO **HA 200 SAETA** (Spain)

A demonstration model Ha 200 in civil markings.

ONE OF THE TWO major aircraft manufacturing companies in Spain, La Hispano-Aviacion S.A. is an associate of Hispano Suiza, well-known armaments producer. In common with Construcciones Aeronauticas S.A. (*see* pp. 21–23) Hispano obtained aircraft production licences from Germany, and became responsible for the manufacture of a large number of Messerschmitt Bf 109 fighters for the Spanish Air Force.

This link with Messerschmitt was strengthened after the end of the War when Professor Willi Messerschmitt moved to Spain and took charge of the Hispano design office. The company's first post-War product was the Ha 100 Triana, a piston-engined advanced trainer which appeared in 1954 and went into production for the Spanish Air Force.

Under Professor Messerschmitt's direction, the Hispano design team then turned its attention to a jet-powered advanced trainer—making use of certain components of the Ha 100, including the wings and tailplane. The new type was designated Ha 200 Saeta (Spanish Air Force E 14) and the prototype made its first flight on August 12, 1955.

Power is provided by two Turboméca Marboré IIA turbojets, mounted side-by-side in the centre fuselage and fed by a nose intake. Immediately inside the intake, the airflow is divided into two ducts, with space between for the nose-wheel well. Main units of the landing gear retract sideways to lie in the wings.

The Marboré engines have short tailpipes to exhaust at the wing trailing edge roots. Pupil and instructor sit in tandem in a pressurized cabin.

After two prototypes of the Saeta had been built and flown, orders were placed by the Spanish Air Force and the following variants have appeared to date:

Ha 200A. Initial production version. Basic equipment standard includes two 7 mm. machine-guns in the nose, with a fixed gun sight in the forward cockpit, and a Marconi radio compass. Oerlikon rockets are usually carried beneath the wings which have four strong-points. Five of the pre-production batch of Saetas were Ha 200As, the remainder being the "B" model. After evaluation, the Spanish Air Force ordered a production batch of 30. The first pre-production model flew on June 6, 1960, followed by the first production aircraft on October 11, 1962.

Ha 200B. Similar to Ha 200A but with different equipment standard, including a 20 mm. Hispano-Suiza cannon in the nose, a Ferranti gyroscopic predictor gun sight and Lear ADF. The pre-production batch of ten was divided equally between "A" and "B" models; no further production of the Ha 200B took place. The first flight was made on July 21, 1960.

Ha 200D. Second production batch for the Spanish Air Force, with detail refinements. Heavier external armament loads can be carried, and Dunlop hydraulic plate brakes have been fitted. The Ha 200D can be fitted with 1,058 lb.s.t. Marboré VI turbojets. Fifty-five have been ordered.

Al Kahira. This is the name (meaning Cairo) of a version of the Ha 200 which is in production at the Helwan Air Works in Egypt. These works were inaugurated in July 1962 and the Al Kahira is the first production work undertaken there.

Span (over tip tanks), 36 ft. 2 in.; length, 29 ft. 3½ in.; height, 10 ft. 8 in.; wing area, 187 sq. ft.; aspect ratio, 6.22; sweepback, 4¼ degrees.
Empty equipped weight, 4,035 lb.; gross weight, 7,385 lb.
Max. speed, 404 m.p.h.; cruising speed, 330 m.p.h.; initial rate of climb, 2,755 ft./min.; service ceiling, 39,360 ft.; take-off distance to 50 ft., 1,740 ft.; landing distance from 50 ft., 2,300 ft.; range, 930 miles at 29,500 ft.

1. *The prototype Ha 200 in its original form.*
2. *The prototype with larger dorsal fin and tip tanks.*
3. *Pre-production models of the Ha 200.*
4. *The first production Ha 200.*

I.A.F. KANPUR (India)

PERSONNEL AT the Indian Air Force Maintenance Command Development Centre at Kanpur designed and built the prototype of a four-seat light utility aircraft in less than five months. Its design was directed by Air Vice-Marshal Harjinder Singh, who is Air Officer Commanding-in-Chief at the Kanpur depot, which is responsible for production in India of the Hawker Siddeley 748.

The light plane, powered by a 190 h.p. Lycoming engine, was known as the Kanpur I. Only one prototype was built, but this was followed in October 1961 by a second prototype called the Kanpur II. Powered by a 250 h.p. Lycoming O-540-A1B5 engine, the Kanpur II included a number of refinements and this version was expected to be put into production for the Indian Air Force.

The Kanpur is a conventional high-wing strut-braced monoplane with accommodation for pilot and three passengers. Provision has been made for crop-spraying equipment to be carried and external fuel tanks can be fitted on the wing bracing struts.

Span, 37 ft. 10 in.; length, 26 ft. 6 in.; height, 7 ft. 6 in.; wing area, 200 sq. ft.; aspect ratio, 6.8.
Empty weight, 1,700 lb.; gross weight, 2,600 lb.
Max. speed, 137 m.p.h.; normal cruising speed, 100 m.p.h.; initial rate of climb, 1,155 ft./min.; service ceiling, 20,500 ft.; take-off distance to 50 ft., 650 ft.; landing distance from 50 ft., 720 ft.; range, 460 miles.

1

2

ILYUSHIN IL-18 (U.S.S.R.)

ONE OF Soviet Russia's best-known—and most successful—turbine-engined transports, the Il-18 is also reported to be in service with the Soviet Air Force. The illustration alongside shows one of the early development aircraft in military markings—probably for Air Force evaluation. Subsequent use of the Il-18 by the Soviet Air Force appears to be on a small scale, most requirements for V.I.P. and personnel transportation being met by Aeroflot with civil-registered aircraft.

The Il-18 was first flown in mid-1957, the prototype being powered by 4,000 e.h.p. Kuznetsov NK-4 turboprops. After comparative trials, the Ivchenko AI-20 engine was chosen for production models. The Il-18 is normally equipped to seat 73–84.

Span, 122 ft. 8½ in.; length, 117 ft. 9 in.; height, 33 ft. 4 in.; wing area, 1,507 sq. ft.; aspect ratio, 10; sweepback, nil.
Empty weight, 61,730 lb.; gross weight, 135,600 lb.
Max. speed, 466 m.p.h.; cruising speed, 380 m.p.h.; take-off distance, 3,940 ft.; landing distance, 2,300 ft.; range, 1,550 miles with max. load; max. range, 2,920 miles.

3

1. *The prototype I.A.F. Kanpur I.*
2. *The I.A.F. Kanpur II prototype.*
3. *An early Ilyushin Il-18 in Soviet Air Force markings.*

LOCKHEED AL.60 (LASA-60) (Italy)

LOCKHEED DEVELOPED their Model 60 light utility transport at the Georgia Division, where prototypes were built, but from the start of the project it was intended that the type would be produced in other countries. Market studies indicated that the domestic U.S. market for an aircraft of this type would not be large enough to justify home production.

South American requirements played a prominent part in establishing the design of the Lockheed 60, which is a six-seater with a cabin large enough to permit a number of alternative arrangements in the utility rôle.

The first prototype was first flown at Marietta, Georgia, on September 15, 1959 and was powered by a 250 h.p. Continental IO-470 engine while the second prototype had a 260 h.p. TSIO-470 with turbo-supercharger for better performance when operating from high elevation airfields.

To handle production, Lockheed set up an associate company in Mexico, Lockheed-Azcarate S.A. Production models were designated LASA-60 and the first flew from San Luis Potosi on March 21, 1961. Only 18 were built by this factory however, and all eventually were acquired by the Mexican Air Force to equip a search and rescue squadron. Plans for the Lockheed 60 to be built also in Argentina were abandoned.

In Europe, a licence to build the Lockheed aeroplane was obtained by Aeronautica Macchi, which now has exclusive manufacturing rights outside the U.S.A. The Italian-built versions are designated AL.60; the first flew on April 19, 1961 and more than 80 had been built by 1964. Versions are as follows:

AL.60B1. Tricycle gear and 250 h.p. Continental O-470-R engine.

AL.60B2. As B1 with 260 h.p. Continental TSIO-470-B engine.

AL.60D3. As B1 with 310 h.p. Continental GIO-470-1 geared engine.

AL.60C4. Tail-wheel gear and 340 h.p. Piaggio-Lycoming GSO-480-B1 engine. The most powerful AL.60, this version was designed to meet an Italian Air Force requirement for an aircraft suitable for rough field operation and paratroop training. The proto-

type flew early in 1963 and others were being built in 1964. Data which follow are for this version.

Span, 39 ft. 4 in.; length, 28 ft. 11½ in.; height, 9 ft. 0½ in.; wing area, 210 sq. ft.; aspect ratio, 7.2; sweepback, nil.
Empty weight, 2,557 lb.; payload, 1,328 lb.; gross weight, 4,500 lb.
Max. speed, 167 m.p.h. at 15,750 ft.; initial rate of climb, 775 ft./min.; service ceiling, 18,040 ft.; take-off distance to 50 ft., 1,225 ft.; landing distance from 50 ft., 807 ft.; range, 500 miles.

1

1. A Lockheed L.60 in Mexican civil markings.
2. A Macchi-built AL.60.
3 The prototype AL.60C4 with combination ski-wheels.

2

3

LOCKHEED C-141 STARLIFTER (U.S.A.)

The first C-141A on an early test flight.

MOST ADVANCED military transport aircraft yet put into production, the Lockheed C-141 was designed to meet an urgent requirement to modernize the airlift capability of the U.S. Military Transport Service. This requirement originated in 1960 with the realization that M.A.T.S. lacked the capability to fulfil its primary mission of strategic transportation as effectively as it might. A Specific Operational Requirement, SOR182, was issued to the U.S. manufacturing industry on May 4, 1960 and four companies, Boeing, Convair, Douglas and Lockheed, submitted bids.

Lockheed was named the winner on March 13, 1961 and three days later procurement authorization was issued for development of the new aircraft to proceed as Support System SS476-L. The Lockheed design was identified as Model 300 and was prepared by the Georgia division of the company. In general configuration—i.e. high-wing, rear-loading, etc.—the Model 300 followed the Hercules pattern, but it was much larger and with a much higher performance, using a sweptback wing and turbojet engines.

When the SOR182 programme was drawn up, an initial requirement for 132 aircraft was established. This figure was more than adequate to justify production of a new type; however, in order to obtain the aircraft at the lowest possible unit cost the U.S.A.F. specified that the transport should be designed for civil as well as military use, provided the major military requirements were not compromised. Tentative airline orders for a long-fuselage commercial version, the L-300B (later L-301), were placed in 1964.

A key factor in arriving at the initial design configuration was the need to load and off-load a very wide range of stores with the minimum of ground equipment. A floor at truck-bed height was essential and this in turn made a high-wing position inevitable. Modest sweepback on the wing gave preference to field performance and slow-speed handling, rather than high-speed cruise. Location of the engines was conditioned by the need to air-drop troops and supplies from the rear-fuselage doors. This made it impossible to use rear-mounted engines, which Lockheed might otherwise have been expected to favour following their

y

selection for the C-140 JetStar (see p. 83). With four engine pods hanging beneath the high-mounted wing, a fuselage-mounted tailplane became impossible, leading to selection of the "T" tail. Location of the main landing gear in fuselage-side blisters was a "natural" in view of Lockheed's experience with this arrangement in the C-130 Hercules.

The C-141 is designed to use the U.S.A.F. 463L mechanical loading system, for which purpose it has roller track down the length of the cabin floor. Over 90 per cent of all air-portable military equipment can be accommodated within the 10 ft. by 9 ft. by 81 ft. cube of the pressurized cabin.

First contracts for the C-141A (the initial production version of the Starlifter) were concluded on August 16, 1961 and covered the first five aircraft. These five aircraft were allocated to the test programme; the first (61-2775) flew on December 17, 1963.

Production contracts for 127 aircraft were signed in 1964 to cover procurement in the 1963, 1964 and 1965 Fiscal Years. The first of these (63-8077) and the two subsequent aircraft were allocated to U.S.A.F. test programmes, with the ninth C-141A (63-8080) earmarked as the first Starlifter for operational use, by the end of 1964.

Span, 160 ft. 0 in.; length, 145 ft. 0 in.; height, 39 ft. 4 in.; wing area, 3,228 sq. ft.; aspect ratio, 7.9; sweepback, 25 degrees.
Empty equipped weight, 134,380 lb.; max. military payload over 70,000 lb.; gross weight, 316,000 lb.; max. landing weight, 257,500 lb.
Cruising speed, 550 m.p.h.; initial rate of climb, 3,400 ft./min.; operating ceiling, 50,000 ft.; take-off distance to 50 ft., 5,300 ft.; landing distance from 50 ft., 3,700 ft.; range with max. payload, 4,163 st. miles; range with max. fuel, 6,244 st. miles.

1. *The C-141A with wheels and flaps down.*
2 and 3. *Two ground views of the first C-141A.*
4. *The ninth Starlifter, first of the type to be delivered to the U.S.A.F., at M.A.T.S. Tinker A.F.B.*

1

2

3

4

y

[79]

LOCKHEED C-130 HERCULES (U.S.A.)

A Lockheed C-130E Hercules in service with M.A.T.S.

AFTER PROLONGED DEBATE and extensive research, the United States Air Force reached a policy decision during 1950 to adopt turboprop engines for a new generation of transport aircraft. As an immediate result of this decision, steps were taken to initiate development of three new aircraft—a tactical transport, a strategic transport and a specialized heavy duty transport. These three types became, respectively, the Lockheed C-130 Hercules, the Douglas C-133 Cargomaster (*see* p. 42) and the Douglas C-132 (which was abandoned before completion).

A design competition for the tactical transport was held early in 1951—the Lockheed entry was dated February 2 in that year—and selection of the Lockheed Model 82 as the winning entry was announced a few months later. The prototype contract was awarded on July 11, 1951.

Key features of the Hercules design were the large fuselage cross-section to accommodate a wide range of military stores, the rear-loading ramp, and the arrangement of the main landing gear in blisters on the fuselage side, to avoid the complication of retracting the gear into the wings or engine nacelles.

As powerplant for the C-130, Lockheed adopted four Allison T56 turboprops, mounted in nacelles fitting under the wing.

The basic Hercules is operated by a flight crew of four and provides accommodation for up to 92 equipped troops, 64 paratroops or 70 stretchers with 6 attendants. As a freighter, it can carry six pallets or various individual items including complete missile systems. The rear-loading ramp can be opened in flight to drop supplies; paratroops leave by doors on each side of the fuselage.

Initial development of the Hercules was undertaken as a complete support system, SS400L, and it was the first transport aircraft to be so developed. Under the unified tri-service designating scheme which became effective in 1962, versions of the Hercules which had gone into service with the U.S. Navy and U.S. Marines were re-designated in the C-130 series applicable to the U.S.A.F. versions. All are described below under their current designations.

YC-130. Two prototypes ordered on July 11, 1951 with 3,750 e.s.h.p. Allison T56-A-1A turboprops. Built at Lockheed California plant, Burbank. First flight August 23, 1954. Gross weight, 108,000 lb.

C-130A. Initial production model. All production models built at Lockheed Georgia plant, Marietta, where the first C-130A flew on April 7, 1955. Basic transport for Tactical Air Command units. Allison T56-A-1A or -9 turboprops with three-blade Aeroproducts propellers. Gross weight, 124,200 lb. All but first few aircraft have weather mapping radar, distinguished by large nose radome. Post-delivery modification permits installation of 450 U.S. gallon external tank under each wing. Total of 219 C-130As built for T.A.C. (first delivered on December 9, 1956 at Ardmore A.F.B., Okla.) plus 12 with T56-A-11 engines for the R.A.A.F. Two C-130As were converted as drone launcher/directors (originally designated GC-130A) and carry up to four Ryan or Northrop drones beneath the wings. The fuselage nose of these two aircraft was lengthened by 30 in. for installation of special drone control and other equipment.

RC-130A. Sixteen aircraft built for service with M.A.T.S. 1,370th Photo Mapping Wing, Air Photographic and Charting Service. Based on C-130A with addition of special photographic and navigation equipment and provision for additional crew members.

C-130B. Second basic transport variant for T.A.C. Principal changes comprised 4,050 e.s.h.p. T56-A-7 turboprops with four-blade Hamilton-Standard propellers, additional fuel (1,710 U.S. gallons) in inner wing tanks, strengthened landing gear and 135,000 lb. gross weight. First flight December 10, 1958. First delivery June 12, 1959. Approximately 150 built for U.S.A.F., plus ten for Indonesian
[*Continued on p. 82*

1. *Early production C-130A without nose radome.*
2. *A GC-130A carrying a Radioplane Q-4B target drone.*
3. *Lockheed C-130B of the R.C.A.F.*
4. *The single C-130C with jet pods.*

LOCKHEED C-130 HERCULES (U.S.A.)

Air Force, four for R.C.A.F., four for Pakistan Air Force and seven for S.A.A.F. Four were supplied to the Imperial Iranian Air Force from the U.S.A.F. in 1962.

HC-130B. Six C-130Bs were modified during 1961 for use on missile range support duties. These duties included the aerial recovery (by snatch technique) of Discoverer and Samos satellites during their descent. Originally designated JC-130B and operated by 6593rd Test Squadron at Hickam A.F.B., Hawaii.

C-130C. One C-130B (also known as NC-130B) was modified to have a boundary layer control system. Two specially adapted Allison YT56-A-6 engines in underwing pods provided compressed air which was blown over the wing and tail control surfaces and flaps to reduce the stalling speed and take-off and landing distances. First flown February 8, 1960.

C-130D. Thirteen C-130As were modified for use by the U.S.A.F. in the Antarctic under this designation. Principal change was to fit skis on the main and nose landing gear; these skis could be raised or lowered when the wheels were down, so that the aircraft could operate from runways or on snow. Another modification allowed hot air to be bled from the engines and used for snow and ice removal from the aircraft while on the ground. Provision for underwing fuel tanks, auxiliary fuel in tanks in cabin and J.A.T.O.

C-130E. Third basic transport variant, developed in 1961 primarily as interim modernization equipment for M.A.T.S. Subsequently ordered also for T.A.C. and export. Principal differences from C-130B are the use of 1,360 U.S. gallon underwing fuel tanks and structural provision for gross weight up to 175,000 lb. to permit long-range strategic airlift missions to be flown. First flight August 25, 1961; first delivery April, 1962. Orders total 235 for M.A.T.S. and T.A.C., three for R.N.Z.A.F.,

and 16 for R.C.A.F. One C-130E has been built as a civil demonstrator.

KC-130F. Variant of the C-130B for the U.S. Marines (originally GV-1), following trials with two C-130As in flight-refuelling rôle. Has 3,600 U.S. gallon tank in cabin and equipment for simultaneous refuelling of two aircraft using probe and drogue method. First flight January 22, 1962; delivery of 46 completed at end of 1962.

C-130F. Seven aircraft used for transport duties by U.S. Navy. Originally designated GV-1U and similar to KC-130F without the refuelling equipment.

LC-130F. Four aircraft (originally C-130BL) used by U.S. Navy for operation in the Antarctic. Based on C-130B but with ski-wheel gear as described above for C-130D.

HC-130G. Twelve aircraft based on C-130B delivered to U.S. Coast Guard in 1962–63 for search and rescue duties (originally SC-130B). Special features include observation stations in the rear cargo compartment and seats on the flight deck for an "on-scene" commander and radio operator in addition to the normal crew of four. Normal interior arrangement provides up to 44 seats.

HC-130H. Variant based on C-130E for use by M.A.T.S. Air Rescue Service. Equipped for air search, rescue and satellite recovery missions. Has 4,510 e.s.h.p. Allison T56-A-15 engines, fuselage length increased by 4 in., provision for 3,600 U.S. gallons of fuel in the cabin and new equipment. First of 63 on order flew on December 8, 1964.

Data for the C-130E:
Span, 132 ft. 7 in.; length, 97 ft. 9 in.; height, 38 ft. 3 in.; wing area, 1,745 sq. ft.; aspect ratio, 10.09; sweepback, nil.
Empty equipped weight, 72,892 lb.; normal gross weight, 155,000 lb.; max. overload take-off weight, 175,000 lb.
Max. speed, 345 m.p.h.; cruising speed, 334 m.p.h.; initial rate of climb, 1,500 ft./min.; service ceiling, 20,000 ft.; take-off distance to 50 ft., 5,800 ft.; landing distance from 50 ft., 2,800 ft.; range, 2,530 miles with max. load, 4,900 miles with max. fuel.

---

5. *Ski-equipped Lockheed C-130D.*
6. *A Marines KC-130F tanker at work.*
7. *One of six HC-130Bs for missile recovery.*
8. *U.S. Coast Guard HC-130G.*

LOCKHEED C-140 JETSTAR (U.S.A.)

DURING 1956, the U.S.A.F. invited the aircraft manufacturing industry to participate in a programme to develop two new types of jet aircraft—a utility transport (UCX) and a utility trainer (UTX).

In the case of the UCX, only Lockheed accepted the terms of the U.S.A.F. offer and developed a suitable aeroplane. This was the Model 1329 JetStar, the prototype of which was built in 241 days after the design had been finalized, to make its first flight on September 4, 1957.

This and a second prototype were initially powered by two Bristol Siddeley Orpheus engines apiece although Lockheed had provided for the JetStar to have four engines of lower power. A rear-engined layout was chosen, the JetStar thus becoming the first U.S.-designed aeroplane to follow the pattern set by the Sud Caravelle. With the wing freed of powerplant extruberances, Lockheed designers were able to design large external tanks which fit right over the wing at the mid-span position. Meeting the UCX specification, the JetStar provided accommodation for up to ten passengers with a crew of two in a flight deck equipped to permit senior staff officers in ground appointments to maintain their flying proficiency.

In October 1959, two years after the JetStar first flew, the U.S.A.F. announced that it would adopt the type for service, with four Pratt & Whitney J60 (JT12A) turbojets, and one of the prototypes re-engined with this powerplant flew in December 1959. The first military order, placed in June 1960, was for five JetStars to be designated C-140A and used by the Airway and Air Communication Service operated World-wide by M.A.T.S. to check and calibrate navigation aids used by U.S.A.F. aircraft.

Subsequently, 11 more JetStars were ordered for use by M.A.T.S.—five as C-140B to be used by the special air missions wing and six VC-140B staff transports. All had been delivered by 1963.

Principal use of the JetStar, despite its military origins, has proved to be in the executive rôle, for which some 60 had been sold by 1964. Other than the U.S.A.F., only Germany had purchased the type for military use, two being operated as staff transports by the Luftwaffe.

The JetStar is structurally conventional, with a fail-safe stressed skin on the wing incorporating extruded skin/stringer sections. Double-slotted flaps and hinged leading edge flaps help to minimize take-off and landing distances. A speed brake is fitted on the underside of the rear fuselage.

Span, 54 ft. 5 in.; length, 60 ft. 5 in.; height, 20 ft. 5 in.; wing area, 542.5 sq. ft.; aspect ratio, 5.27; sweepback, 30 degrees.
Empty equipped weight, 21,500 lb.; gross weight, 40,900 lb.
Max. speed, 574 m.p.h. at 23,000 ft.; cruising speed, 495 m.p.h. at 40,000 ft.; initial rate of climb, 3,300 ft./min.; service ceiling, 33,000 ft.; take-off distance to 50 ft., 4,275 ft.; landing distance from 50 ft., 3,300 ft.; range, 1,980 miles with max. payload.

1. *A JetStar in Luftwaffe colours.*
2. *A Lockheed C-140A of the U.S.A.F. Air Force Communications Service.*
3. *A VC-140B staff transport in M.A.T.S. colours.*

MACCHI **MB326** (Italy)

A Macchi MB326 in service with the Italian Air Force.

IN PRODUCTION SINCE 1960 for the Italian Air Force, the Aeronautica Macchi MB326 is one of the many types of basic jet trainers which have been produced in the past decade in efforts to simplify pilot training and to reduce the number of aircraft types needed. It falls into the same category as several other types described in this volume, including the Hunting Jet Provost (pp. 71–73), Cessna T-37 (pp. 24–25), Canadair CL-41 (pp. 18–19) and others.

Following the dictates of the Italian Air Force specification which was issued in 1954, Macchi adopted tandem seating for the pupil and instructor. In this respect, the MB326 differs from the basic jet trainer adopted for service in the U.S., Canada, Great Britain and numerous other countries, which favour side-by-side seating.

Power for the MB326 is provided by a 2,500 lb.s.t. Bristol Siddeley Viper ASV.11 turbojet, installed at the rear of the centre fuselage section. The rear fuselage section can be removed completely to permit the engine to be changed. No fuel is carried in the wing, the fuselage tank (between the cockpit and the engine) being supplemented by the two tip tanks. The engine air intakes are at the wing roots but just proud of the fuselage side to avoid the turbulent boundary layer of air.

Two prototypes of the MB326 were ordered by the Italian Air Force and actual construction began during 1956. The first prototype flew on December 10, 1957 and was powered by a Viper ASV.8. The Viper ASV.11 was first fitted in the second prototype, and engines for the production models are produced under licence by IAM Rinaldo Piaggio Sp.A. Variants of the basic type are as follows:

MB326. Production model for the Italian Air Force, which ordered 100. First production aircraft flew on October 5, 1960 and delivery to Flying Schools began in January 1962. Italian Air Force pilots receive the first 150 hours (approx.) of their training on this type. Orders were also placed for seven by the Ghana Air Force and for eight by the Tunisian Air Force.

MB326B. Projected single-seat ground attack version. An MB326 has been used to develop the underwing stores for this version, carried on six underwing stations. A gun or camera pod can be carried on each inner station; all six stations can carry a general purpose pylon for a 260 lb. bomb or two HVAR 5-in. rockets on each. Air-to-ground or air-to-air missiles can be carried, or ferry tanks; total underwing load is 2,100 lb. The aircraft can also be used to tow a sleeve or Del Mar target for air-to-air firing.

MB326C. Projected navigation and radar trainer with provision to carry the NASARR radar equipment used in the Italian Air Forces F-104G Starfighters. The MB326C would be powered by a 3,000 lb.s.t. Viper 20 turbojet and would have a lengthened nose to accommodate the special electronic equipment.

MB326D. Six aircraft acquired by Alitalia for *ab initio* training of airline pilots, with suitable electronic and navigation equipment.

Span, 34 ft. 8 in. (over tip tanks); length, 34 ft. 11¼ in.; height, 12 ft. 2½ in.; wing area, 205 sq. ft.; aspect ratio, 5.26; sweepback, nil.

Empty weight, 4,930 lb.; gross weight, 7,347 lb. (MB326B, 9,480 lb.).

Max. speed, 501 m.p.h. at 20,000 ft.; initial rate of climb, 4,500 ft./min.; service ceiling, 44,000 ft.; take-off distance to 50 ft., 1,950 ft.; landing distance from 50 ft., 2,100 ft.; range with max. fuel, 690 miles at 36,000 ft.

1

2

3

1. *The prototype Macchi MB326.*
2. *A production model MB326.*
3. *The armed MB326 with underwing rockets and gun pods.*
4. *An MB326D in Alitalia markings.*

4

M-4 TARPAN (Poland)

POLAND'S AIRCRAFT INDUSTRY, responsible for a number of well-known aeroplanes before World War II under the PZL imprint, is now a State-controlled enterprise, with three principal factories. These factories, at Warsaw-Okecie, Mielec and Swidnik, each have a design organization and several types of aircraft of original Polish design are under development in addition to Soviet types built under licence.

Latest product of the Mielec factory is the M-4 Tarpan, a two-seat basic trainer for civil or military use. A prototype flew on September 7, 1961 and production began in 1962. Deliveries have been made to flying schools training military and civil pilots, and to Polish aero clubs.

The Tarpan is powered by a 180 h.p. Narkiewicz WN-6 piston engine, and is available in several versions. In addition to the basic M-4 there is the M-4P equipped with special navigation equipment for all-weather flying, and the M-4A, a single-seater for advanced aerobatic flying.

Span, 29 ft. 1 in.; length, 24 ft. 1 in.; height, 9 ft. 0 in.; wing area, 127 sq. ft.; aspect ratio, 6.56; sweepback, nil.
Empty equipped weight, 1,671 lb.; gross weight, 2,315 lb.
Max. speed, 191 m.p.h.; initial rate of climb, 1,260 ft.; service ceiling, 22,640 ft.; take-off distance to 50 ft., 1,510 ft.; landing distance from 50 ft., 1,445 ft.; max. range, 466 miles.

MALMO MFI-10 VIPAN (Sweden)

FIRST ORIGINAL design completed by the AB Malmo Flygindustri of Malmo, Sweden, is the Vipan (Peewit) light liaison and utility aircraft. It is now being developed under the direction of the chief of the company's Aircraft Division, Mr. Bjorn Andreasson. Mr. Andreasson had previously designed a number of aircraft in the U.S.A. and one of these is also in production by Malmo as the MFI-9 Junior.

The prototype MFI-10 with a 160 h.p. Lycoming O-320 engine, was first flown in 1961 and was a civil model. Two MFI-10Bs were built under Swedish Army contract for evaluation, with 180 h.p. Lycoming O-360 engines, and the first of these flew on June 27, 1962.

Span, 35 ft. 2½ in.; length, 25 ft. 11 in.; height, 7 ft. 2¾ in.; wing area, 169 sq. ft.; aspect ratio, 7.35; sweepback, nil.
Empty equipped weight, 1,433 lb.; gross weight, 2,590 lb.
Max. speed, 146 m.p.h.; cruising speed, 137 m.p.h.; initial rate of climb, 670 ft./min.; service ceiling, 14,000 ft.; take-off run, 590 ft.; range with max. fuel, 620 miles.

1. The prototype Tarpan.
2. A Tarpan in civil markings.
3. Second prototype MFI-10 in Swedish Army colours.

MILES STUDENT (Great Britain)

THE STUDENT was produced in 1957 as a private venture by F. G. Miles Ltd. and was the first original design by the company which succeeded the well-known Miles Aircraft Ltd. Intended for use primarily as a basic jet trainer, the M.100 Student incorporated a number of distinctive design features which distinguished it from the large number of more conventional jet trainers described in this volume.

A high wing position was adopted, with a small amount of wing sweepback to give a good top performance. The engine was located high on the fuselage behind the cockpit, with an N.A.C.A.-type flush inlet. This arrangement made it possible to keep down the overall height, improving rough-field handling and reducing the effects of cross-wind. Side-by-side seating was adopted, with provision for two additional passenger seats if the aircraft was needed in the communications rôle.

The Student prototype has been tested in two forms and has given rise to further projected variants as noted below:

Student 1. The prototype in its original form, powered by an 880 lb.s.t. Turboméca Marboré 2A engine. First flown (as G-45-1) on May 14, 1957 and later registered G-APLK.

Student 2. The prototype Student was modified in 1963–64 to demonstrate its adaptability for the ground-attack or counter-insurgency rôle. It was re-engined with a 1,050 lb. Marboré 6F turbojet and many detail changes were made in the light of several years' flying experience. For armament trials, a strong point was introduced in each wing, to carry a weapon pod or camera installation. With an 0.303-in. machine-gun pod under each wing and re-numbered XS941, the Student 2 first flew on April 22, 1964 and subsequently underwent gunnery trials.

Graduate. Projected definitive version, with the same dimensions as the Student but powered by a 1,540 lb.s.t. Turboméca Aubisque turbofan. This would have additional wing strong points for rockets or bombs, and wing-tip mounts for tanks or napalm bombs.

Centurion. Projected five-seat civil or military communications version with one or two engines.

Span, 29 ft. 0 in.; length, 27 ft. 0 in.; height, 6 ft. 6 in.; wing area, 144 sq. ft.; aspect ratio, 5.86; sweepback, 15 degrees.
Empty equipped weight, 2,400 lb.; gross weight, 3,900 lb.
Max. speed, 313 m.p.h.; cruising speed, 233 m.p.h.; initial rate of climb, 2,250 ft./min.; take-off distance to 50 ft., 1,920 ft.; landing distance from 50 ft., 1,920 ft.; range, 455 miles with full load.

1

2

3

1. *The Student in its original form as G-35-4.*
2. *The Student registered G-APLK, showing the tip tanks.*
3. *The Student 2, as XS941, with underwing armament.*

NAMC YS-11 (Japan)

MILITARY VERSIONS of Japan's first post-War airliner have been ordered for use as troop-transports and other versions have been projected for Service use. Development of the basic YS-11 design began in 1957, with the object of producing a medium-range transport for the domestic airline market and for export.

As no single aircraft manufacturing company in Japan at that time had adequate technical resources to undertake such a programme, the Japanese Government encouraged formation of a consortium of six companies. These companies set up a Transport Aircraft Development Association to establish the overall design, and then formed the Nihon Aeroplane Manufacturing Co. to undertake its manufacture.

The YS-11 is a conventional twin-engined low-wing monoplane. The engines are Rolls-Royce Dart R.Da.10/1 Mk. 542s rated at 3,060 e.h.p. each—almost twice the power of the Darts used in the four-engined Vickers Viscount, which is of similar size to the YS-11. Normal accommodation, in the airline version of the YS-11, is for up to 60 passengers, four-abreast.

The first of two prototypes of the YS-11 (JA8611) flew on August 30, 1962, followed by the second (JA8612) on December 28, 1962. Test flying was completed by mid-1964 and a certificate of airworthiness was obtained on August 25. Delivery of production aircraft began in the Spring of 1965, and the YS-11 entered commercial airline service with Toa Airways on April 1. Other early production aircraft were delivered to All-Nippon Airways and to Japan Domestic Airways.

Military versions of the aircraft include the YS-11P personnel transport and an ECM variant. The YS-11P retains most of the features of the airline version, but carries additional or changed electronic equipment. The basic cabin arrangement provides for 32 seats; use of a moveable bulkhead permits mixed loads of passengers and freight to be carried. For V.I.P. use, a lounge with two settee beds can be installed. In the casualty evacuation rôle, the YS-11P carries six stretchers and eight seats.

Four YS-11Ps have been ordered by the Japanese Air Self-Defence Force and one by the Japanese Maritime Self-Defence Force. Plans to purchase the electronic countermeasures version have been delayed by slow development of the ECM equipment.

1. *The first prototype YS-11 in flight.*
2. *The second YS-11, JA8612.*
3. *The first YS-11, JA8611.*

Span, 104 ft. 11½ in.; length, 86 ft. 3½ in.; height, 29 ft. 9 in.; wing area, 1,020 sq. ft.; aspect ratio, 10.8; sweepback, nil.
Empty weight, 32,928 lb.; gross weight, 51,800 lb.
Max. cruising speed, 296 m.p.h. at 20,000 ft.; initial rate of climb, 1,520 ft./min.; service ceiling, 27,500 ft.; take-off field length, 3,115 ft.; landing field length, 3,905 ft.; range, 390 miles with full load, 1,485 miles with max. fuel.

NORD 3202 (France)

TWO PROTOTYPES were built in 1953–54 of a replacement for the Stampe trainer biplane—the Nord N.3200 (F-WGVS) with a 260 h.p. Salmson-Argus 8AS-04, first flown on September 10, 1954; and the Nord N.3201 (F-WGVL) with a 170 h.p. SNECMA-Regnier 4 LO 2 engine, first flown on June 22, 1954.

The French Army Air Corps (*Aviation Légère de l'Armée de Terre*) ordered 100 of the N.3202 variant, a prototype of which flew on April 17, 1957. Deliveries began in July 1959: 50 were powered by the 240 h.p. Potez 4D 32 engine and 50 by the 260 h.p. Potez 4D 34B.

Span, 31 ft. 2 in.; length, 26 ft. 8 in.; height, 9 ft. 3 in.; wing area, 175 sq. ft.; aspect ratio, 5.5; sweepback, nil.
Empty equipped weight, 1,896 lb.; gross weight, 2,690 lb.
Max. speed, 161 m.p.h.; cruising speed, 135 m.p.h.; initial rate of climb, 1,310 ft./min.; range, 560 miles.

NORD 3400 (France)

THE NORD 3400 was designed to meet a 1956 specification for a light observation aircraft for A.L.A.T., the French Army Air Corps. A design tender was accepted on January 11, 1957.

Manufacture of the prototypes began in March 1957 and the first flights of these two aircraft were made, respectively, on January 20, 1958 and September 13, 1958. Production orders followed and the first of 150 Nord 3400s reached the French Army on July 9, 1959. Power is supplied by a 260 h.p. Potez 4D 34 in-line inverted engine.

Span, 43 ft. 0 in.; length, 27 ft. 9 in.; height, 10 ft. 3 in.; wing area, 224 sq. ft.; aspect ratio, 8.24; sweepback, nil.
Empty equipped weight, 2,205 lb.; max. gross weight, 3,200 lb.
Cruising speed, 132 m.p.h. at 6,400 ft.; initial rate of climb, 1,180 ft./min.; max. range, 840 miles.

NORD 2501 NORATLAS (France)

A Nord 2501 Noratlas of the French Air Force.

IN SERVICE with four Air Forces, the Noratlas was phased out of production in 1964, 14 years after the first flight of the prototype. Developed to meet a French Air Force requirement for a tactical transport to replace the Junkers Ju 52/3ms and Douglas C-47s in service at the end of the war, the Noratlas was subsequently adopted as standard equipment by the resurgent Luftwaffe in West Germany, where a second production line was established. In addition to its service in France and Germany, the Noratlas has gone into service in small numbers with the air forces of Israel and Portugal.

Basic missions for the Noratlas included transportation of heavy freight loads and air-dropping of supplies and personnel. Nord adopted a configuration similar to that of the Fairchild C-82, with a short, capacious fuselage ending in split-opening doors for rear loading, and the tail unit carried on twin booms extending aft from the engine nacelles. Two piston-engines were adopted for best reliability and economy at the time the project was conceived, in 1947.

Loads carried by the Noratlas can include 45 equipped troops, 36 paratroops or 18 stretchers with attendants, or a variety of wheeled and tracked vehicles. A 2-ton winch can be attached to tie-down points in the cabin floor and used to help loading of heavy cargo in conjunction with a roller at the door sill.

The rear doors of the Noratlas cannot be opened in flight, but they can be completely removed and replaced by an open-ended fairing if it is required to operate the aircraft for air-dropping of heavy supplies or tail-gating by paratroops. The normal paratroop door is in the port side of the rear fuselage.

Crew complement of the Noratlas comprises five—two pilots, navigator, radio operator and flight engineer. The structural design is simple and straightforward, both wings and fuselage being all-metal stressed-skin components.

Development of the Noratlas has produced the following variants:

Nord 2500. Original prototype (F-WFKL) flown for the first time on September 10, 1949. Powered by two 1,600 h.p. Gnome-Rhone 14R piston radial engines.

Nord 2501. Basic production version. The second prototype Noratlas, first flown on November 30, 1950, was the prototype N.2501 and was followed by three pre-production aircraft, the first of which flew in September 1952. Powered by two 2,040 h.p. SNECMA-built Bristol Hercules radial engines—either Mk. 738 (non-reversing propellers, no torque-meter), Mk. 739 (non-reversing propellers, torquemeters fitted), Mk. 758 (reversing propellers, no torquemeter) or Mk. 759 (reversing propellers, torquemeters fitted). Delivery of the initial batch of 40 was completed on June 25, 1954; by December 1957, 154 had been delivered and a total of 211 was eventually delivered to the French Air Force.

The Noratlas was still serving as the principal French transport, equipping eight squadrons of the CoTAM (Transport Command), at the end of 1964.

When the Noratlas was selected for use by the Luftwaffe, a consortium of three German companies was formed to handle its production. These companies were HFB, Siebelwerke and Weser and the consortium was called Flug-zeugbau Nord GmbH, or Nordflug. The first Nordflug 2501 flew on August 6, 1958 and orders eventually totalled 160, with production ending in 1964. In addition 25 Nord-built N.2501s were delivered to the Luftwaffe, as well as two N.2508s (*see below*).

Nord 2502. Developed particularly for civil operations, the Nord 2502 was distinguished by the wing-tip mounted Turboméca Marboré turbojets which provided an additional reserve of power for take-off. First flight, June 1, 1955. Examples were purchased by UAT and Air Algerie for civil operation, but six of UAT's seven Nord 2502s later went to the Portuguese Air Force. Six more were purchased by the Israeli Air Force and in 1962, the Portuguese

[*Continued on p. 92*

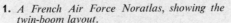

1. *A French Air Force Noratlas, showing the twin-boom layout.*
2. *Ground view of a French Air Force Noratlas.*
3. *Troops embark in a Luftwaffe Noratlas.*
4. *An Israeli Air Force Noratlas.*

NEIVA L-6 PAULISTINHA (Brazil)

SOCIEDADE CONSTRUTORA AERONAUTICA NEIVA in Brazil has been responsible for the production of a series of lightplanes and sailplanes of original design for military and commercial use.

The first Neiva lightplane was the Paulistinha 56, similar in appearance and performance to the Piper Super Cub and originally produced as the C.A.P.4 in 1942 by the Companhia Aeronautica Paulista.

A version of the Paulistinha was ordered for liaison and observation duties with the Brazilian Air Force and continues in service although it is no longer in production. This type, with the Air Force designation L-6, had a 100 h.p. Lycoming and modifications to improve the view from the rear seat. Pilot and observer sat in tandem and the necessary specialized equipment was provided.

To the designs of the research and development division (I.P.D.) of the State-owned Centro Tecnico de Aeronautica, Neiva produced an improved lightplane of similar configuration to the Paulistinha. This was the IPD 5802 Campeiro, powered by a 150 h.p. Lycoming O-320 and equipped to operate in the liaison, training, observation and rescue rôles. Primarily intended for military duties, the Campeiro was ordered in 1962 by the Brazilian Air Force which placed a contract for 20 with the designation L-7.

Third in the series of Neiva military lightplanes, the Regente was also designed at the IPD and introduces a nose-wheel undercarriage. It is powered by a 145 h.p. Continental O-300 with a 180 h.p. Lycoming O-360-A1A as an alternative and seats four. The Brazilian Air Force has ordered about 60 designated L-8 and the Brazilian Army has ordered 20 for its Air Observation Squadron.

Data follow for the L-6, which is illustrated:
Span, 35 ft. 3½ in.; length, 22 ft. 2 in.; wing area, 183 sq. ft.
Empty weight, 882 lb.; gross weight, 1,455 lb.
Max. cruising speed, 99 m.p.h.; initial rate of climb, 785 ft./min.; service ceiling, 19,685 ft.; range, 560 miles.

NORD 2501 NORATLAS (France)
[Contined from p. 91]

Air Force ordered another six from Sud, with the designation Nord 2502F.

Nord 2503. A prototype Noratlas powered by Pratt & Whitney R-2800-CB-17 engines. Not produced in quantity.

Nord 2504. A version of the Nord 2502 equipped to serve the French Navy as a flying class-room for anti-submarine operations. Five built. First flown, November 17, 1958.

Nord 2505. Projected military patrol version of Nord 2502, with larger fuselage cross-section.

Nord 2506. A further refinement of the Nord 2502, with modifications to improve field performance and "loadability". These included the use of slotted flaps, air-brakes, low pressure tyres and "kneeling" main legs to bring the fuselage closer to the ground for loading and unloading. The prototype flew in 1957 but no production took place, a planned contract being cancelled in 1957 as part of a cut-back in defence expenditure.

Nord 2507. Projected air-sea search and rescue version of the Nord 2502, with a flight crew of five and seven observers in the cabin. Observation station in rear fuselage, and side blisters.

Nord 2508. Versions of the Nord 2503 with the addition of Turboméca Marboré turbojets in wing-tip pods. Two prototypes were built, and these were sold to the Luftwaffe in 1963, for use as test-beds for equipment for the Transall C.160 (*see* pp. 114–115). First flight, May 29, 1957.

Data for the Nord 2501 *follow:*
Span, 106 ft. 7 in.; length, 72 ft. 0 in.; height, 19 ft. 8 in.; wing area, 1,089 sq. ft.; aspect ratio, 10.5; sweepback, nil.
Empty equipped weight, 28,756 lb.; max. gross weight, 50,700 lb.
Max. speed, 250 m.p.h.; cruising speed, 208 m.p.h. at 9,840 ft.; initial rate of climb, 1,230 ft./min.; service ceiling, 24,600 ft.; take-off distance to 50 ft., 2,680 ft.; landing distance from 50 ft., 2,650 ft.; range, 1,550 miles.

NORTH AMERICAN T-2 BUCKEYE (U.S.A.)

WINNER OF A 1956 design competition, the North American Buckeye was phased out of production at the end of 1960 but was put back into production in 1963 in revised form. The decision by the U.S. Navy to resume procurement of the Buckeye after a three-year gap emphasized its satisfaction with the in-service performance of the initial batch.

The Buckeye was designed, in accordance with the U.S. Navy's requirements, to cover the whole range of flying instructions from *ab initio* to carrier indoctrination. This meant that the aircraft should have good handling qualities, especially on the approach, as well as a reasonably good high speed performance and aerobatic capability.

To trim development costs and achieve good reliability from the start, North American adopted proven components and equipment wherever possible. The wing design derived from that of the FJ-1 Fury and the control system was basically similar to that of the T-28C. Tandem seating was provided for the two occupants, with the cockpit located above the bifurcated intake ducts leading to the single Westinghouse J34-WE-36 turbojet. For armament training, underwing strong points can carry gun pods, bombs, or rocket packs.

An initial order for 26 Buckeyes was placed, the original designation of T2J-1 being later changed to T-2A. The first flight was made on February 10, 1958. The final production total was 217 and these aircraft are used primarily at the U.S. Naval Air Basic Training Command at Pensacola, Florida.

During 1961, North American proposed a new Buckeye variant in which two 3,000 lb.s.t. Pratt & Whitney J60-P-6 turbojets, side-by-side in the rear fuselage, replaced the obsolete J34 engine. Two prototypes were ordered as T2J-2 (later T-2B) and the first of these flew on August 30, 1962. North American (Columbus Division) zero level ejection seats are fitted, and the T-2B retains the ability to cover

a wide range of training details from a pupil's first flight to advanced training and fighter tactics.

An initial production order for ten T-2Bs was placed in March 1964 with a follow-on order for 36 at the end of the year. The first production model of the T-2B flew for the first time at Columbus on May 21, 1965. Data which follow are for this version:

Span, 37 ft. 10¼ in.; length, 38 ft. 3½ in.; height, 14 ft. 9½ in.; wing area, 255 sq. ft.; sweepback, nil.
Empty weight, 8,474 lb.; gross weight, 12,316 lb.
Max. speed, 540 m.p.h. at 25,000 ft.; initial rate of climb (single engine), 535 ft./min.; service ceiling, 44,400 ft.; range, 950 miles.

1. *The prototype T-2J1 at Columbus.*
2. *A production model T2-A with cockpit open.*
3. *The first T-2B in flight.*

NORTH AMERICAN **T-39** (U.S.A.)

An early production North American T-39A.

THE T-39 SABRELINER was one of two aeroplanes developed in the late 'fifties under a unique U.S.A.F. scheme to minimize development costs. Under this plan, the U.S. industry was invited to design and build prototypes at its own expense to meet official requirements, with no guarantee that production orders would follow. Thus, the U.S.A.F. would be given the opportunity to evaluate aircraft designed to its specification, with no obligation to buy them.

Two requirements were involved in the plan: one for a jet utility transport (the UCX, which produced the Lockheed JetStar—*see* page 83), and the other for a small jet "combat readiness" trainer (the UTX). Two manufacturers undertook to build UTX prototypes, the North American decision to do so being announced on August 27, 1956, four weeks after the U.S.A.F. had issued its requirement.

North American had begun private venture development of a small jet transport earlier in 1956 and initially favoured a buried engine installation in the wing roots. This layout was changed to a rear-engined arrangement during the detailed design stage, which was completed during 1957.

North American built the prototype NA246 (N4060K) from scratch in approximately ten months, completing it in May 1958. Nonavailability of the 2,500 lb.s.t. General Electric J85 turbojets delayed the first flight, however, until September 16, 1958. The aircraft was named Sabreliner and was evaluated by the U.S.A.F. in the latter months of 1958, leading to an initial order for seven. Three military models have been produced, as follows:

T-39A. Basic U.S.A.F. version for use as a utility trainer. Differences from prototype include use of 3,000 lb.s.t. Pratt & Whitney J60-P-3 turbojets, a lengthened nose to accommodate equipment, and changes in internal layout. The first flight of the first production T-39A was made on June 30, 1960, by which time 42 were on order. Subsequent contracts brought total procurement to 143, for use by U.S.A.F. Air Training Command, Strategic Air Command, Systems Command, Headquarters and M.A.T.S. Deliveries began in June 1961 and were complete by 1964.

North American type number allocation was NA265 for the first 88 aircraft and NA276 for the final 55.

T-39B. Six aircraft in the initial production batch—actually the sixth to eleventh machines in the sequence—were completed for special duties at Nellis A.F.B. in the training of F-105 Thunderchief pilots. They carry NASARR, the North American Search and Ranging Radar for all-weather use which is installed in the F-105. Doppler navigation equipment is also fitted. The T-39B was the first version of the design to enter service, the first aircraft being delivered to Tactical Air Command on February 15, 1961. North American designation is NA270.

T-39C. Designation reserved for proposed ECM and strategic bomber radar operator trainer variant.

T-39D. Originally designated T3J-1, this is a U.S. Navy version. Forty-two were ordered, primarily to be used in maritime radar indoctrination training, for which purpose they have a Magnavox radar system fitted. Deliveries began in August 1963, to the Naval Air Training Command at Pensacola. North American give the designation NA277 to the initial 32 and NA285 to the second batch of ten.

Span, 44 ft. 5 in.; length, 43 ft. 9 in.; height, 16 ft. 0 in.; wing area, 342.5 sq. ft.; sweepback, 28 degrees 30 minutes.
Empty equipped weight, 9,257 lb.; gross weight, 17,760 lb.
Max. cruising speed, 502 m.p.h. at 43,500 ft.; cruising speed, 426 m.p.h. at 35,000 ft.; service ceiling (one engine), 21,500 ft.; take-off distance to 35 ft., 3,500 ft.; landing distance from 50 ft., 2,650 ft.; max. range, 1,950 miles.

1. *The prototype NA246 Sabreliner, N4060K.*
2. *The first production T-39A, 59-2868, at the end of its first flight.*
3. *Second production T-39A, 59-2869.*
4. *Ground view of a T-39A, showing airstairs.*

1

2

3

4

NORTHROP T-38 TALON (U.S.A.)

Northrop T-38As in U.S.A.F. service.

DEVELOPMENT OF THE T-38 Talon, the first supersonic trainer designed as such, sprang from Northrop studies into the total costs of modern military aircraft over their whole service life. These studies showed that the most important cost factor was not the initial research and development costs, as was widely believed, nor even production costs, but the costs of maintenance and operation. Increasing aircraft complexity tended to increase still further the share of the total life costs which were attributable to maintenance and operation.

These considerations led Northrop to embark upon a series of design studies for a low-cost manned weapon system and several fighter and two-seat trainer designs emerged. Northrop reviewed the future needs of European and Asian countries for military aircraft and completed designs for a tactical fighter-bomber and a related two-seat trainer, designated N156F and N156T.

Design development of these types was continued as a private venture until the U.S.A.F. issued a General Operational Requirement for a supersonic basic trainer support system (SS-420L). Northrop were able to meet this GOR with a variant of the N156T proposal and for two years (1957–58) development of the trainer took precedence over the fighter.

A U.S.A.F. contract covering prototype aircraft was placed with Northrop at the end of 1956, when the new aircraft was designated T-38A. Power was provided by two General Electric J85 engines which develop, in the GE-5 model used in production T-38As, 3,850 lb.s.t. each.

The first Talon flew on April 10, 1959 and like the second aircraft had YJ85-GE-1 engines without afterburners. Four more trials aircraft, also designated YT-38, had 3,600 lb. YJ85-GE-5s.

Production contracts for T-38As were first placed in 1959 and the first production aircraft flew in May 1960. Subsequent contracts brought the total on order by 1964 to 634. Deliveries to the U.S.A.F. began on March 17, 1961 with the first aircraft going to the 3510th Flying Training Wing at Randolph A.F.B.

With the Talon programme under way, Northrop initiated prototype construction of the single-seat N156F and early in 1959 obtained U.S. Government funding to cover three flying prototypes and a static test specimen. The first N156F flew on July 30, 1959 and was quickly followed by the second; the third was not flown until May 1963, by which time it had been modified to full production standard as an F-5A, following adoption of the N156F, in April 1962, as an all-purpose fighter to be supplied to U.S. allies under the Mutual Aid Programme. This programme, initially covering nearly 200 aircraft for seven nations, includes two-seat F-5B trainers in the ratio of approximately one for every nine F-5As. The first F-5B flew on February 24, 1964.

As a two-seat counterpart of the F-5A, the F-5B has numerous differences from the T-38A, as well as many similarities. The powerplant consists of two 4,080 lb.s.t. J85-GE-13 engines and there are structural differences, notably in the wing. The F-5B also retains the single-seat fighter's external store capability up to a maximum of 6,200 lb. and has two 20 mm. guns in the nose. Pilot and ground crew training on F-5Bs began at Williams A.F.B. in mid-1964.

Data for the T-38A follow:
Span, 25 ft. 3 in.; length, 46 ft. 4½ in.; height, 12 ft. 10½ in.; wing area, 170 sq. ft.; aspect ratio, 3.75; sweepback, nil.
Empty weight, 7,146 lb.; gross weight, 11,700 lb.
Max. speed, Mach.=1.3 (840 m.p.h. at 36,000 ft.); cruising speed. Mach.=0.88; initial rate of climb, 32,500 ft./min.; service ceiling, 53,500 ft.; take-off distance to 50 ft., 3,850 ft.; landing distance from 50 ft., 5,650 ft.; range, 1,140 miles with max. fuel.

1

2

3

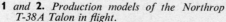

1 *and* **2.** *Production models of the Northrop T-38A Talon in flight.*
3. *A T-38A in landing configuration.*
4. *A Northrop F-5B, two-seat version of the F-5A fighter.*

4

OMNIPOL **L 29 DELFIN** (Czechoslovakia)

DEVELOPMENT OF THE L 29 at the Letnany works of the State-owned aircraft industry in Czechoslovakia began in 1957 to meet a requirement for a jet basic trainer to be used by the Warsaw Pact countries. The same requirement led to production of the TS-11 Iskra in Poland (p. 113) and the Yak-30 in Russia. Competitive evaluation of the three types led to selection of the L 29 for service with the Soviet Air Force rather than the indigenous Yak-30 and large scale production of the L 29 was initiated to meet the Soviet and Czech requirements. A quantity of L 29s was ordered by the Syrian Air Force in 1964 and others have been supplied to Indonesia.

In general concept, the L 29 closely follows contemporary practice for jet trainers, its most unusual feature being the "T" tail. Design was directed by Zdenek Rublic and Karel Tomas, well-known in Czechoslavakia, and the first prototype was completed in 1959, flying for the first time on April 5 in that year. This prototype XL 29 was powered by an imported Bristol Siddeley Viper, but the next L 29, flown in July 1960, had an M701 turbo-jet of Czech design and construction, and this unit is standardized in the production aircraft. During 1961, the production prototype of the L 29 was completed and flown and production deliveries from the Kunovice factory began in the spring of 1963. The Soviet and Czech Air Forces apparently shared initial deliveries, with the first L 29s going to Russia in May 1963.

The M701 turbojet is a centrifugal type with a static take-off thrust of 1,900 lb. Fuel is carried in two fuselage tanks and provision is made for drop tanks beneath each wing. The landing gear is hydraulically actuated, the main wheels retracting inwards into the wings and the nosewheel forwards into the fuselage.

No provision is made for fixed armament but the L 29 can carry, on two underwing pylons, two bombs of up to 220 lb. each or four air-to-ground rockets or similar loads.

Span, 34 ft. 0 in.; length, 35 ft. 5 in.; height, 10 ft. 3 in.; wing area, 213 sq. ft.; aspect ratio, 5.36; sweepback, nil.
Empty equipped weight, 5,000 lb.; gross weight (clean), 7,250 lb.; gross weight (underwing stores), 7,800 lb.
Max. speed, 407 m.p.h. at 16,500 ft.; initial climb rate, 2,800 ft./min.; service ceiling, 36,000 ft.; take-off distance to 80 ft., 3,600 ft.; landing distance from 80 ft., 2,900 ft.; range (clean), 400 miles at 16,500 ft.; range (with drop tanks), 560 miles at 16,500 ft.

1

2

3

1. *A production L 29 in Soviet Air Force service.*
2. *The second prototype Delfin.*
3. *A prototype Delfin showing underwing tanks.*

PIAGGIO P.136 and P.166 (Italy)

ONE OF ITALY'S most respected aircraft manufacturers, Rinaldo Piaggio SpA has been engaged in the design and production of military and civil aircraft since 1916. Its first product after the end of World War II was a light transport amphibian, the P.136.

Layout of the P.136 included a flying-boat type hull with a high-mounted gull-type wing and two piston engines driving pusher propellers. Main wheels of the landing gear retracted into the sides of the hull and the tail wheel hinged up behind the end of the hull's planing surface. Accommodation was provided for five in the cabin.

The prototype P.136 flew on August 29, 1948 and the type went into production with 215 h.p. Franklin 6A8-215-139F engines. Production of the P.136 was almost equally divided between civil customers and the Italian Air Force. The latter purchased 18 of the initial production series for general communications duties, followed by another 15 P.136-Ls powered by 270 h.p. Lycoming GO-480-B engines.

From the P.136, Piaggio developed the P.166 light transport, which dispensed with the amphibian capability and the flying-boat hull, but retained similar overall lines. A prototype of the P.166 first flew on November 26, 1957 and production began in 1958. Powerplant comprises two 380 h.p. Lycoming IGSO-540-A1C piston engines.

An order for 21 Piaggio P.166s was placed by the Italian Air Force, for operation in the communications rôle and in support of the Fiat G.91 tactical support squadrons in the field. The military version is designated P.166M and incorporates several modifications, including an enlarged door in the port fuselage side to permit loading of large items of freight. This feature was to meet Air Force requirements, which included the transportation of spare Orpheus turbojets for the Fiat G.91s.

In keeping with the freight carrying rôle, the P.166M has a strengthened floor, incorporating lashing points. Full dual control is provided in the cockpit, and the normal layout in the communications rôle included four individual seats in the main cabin and two additional bench-type seats in the rear radio compartment. Stretchers can replace the seats in the casualty evacuation version of the P.166M, and provision is made for mounting aerial survey cameras.

Span, 46 ft. 9 in.; length, 38 ft. 1 in.; height, 16 ft. 5 in.; wing area, 286 sq. ft.; aspect ratio, 7.3; sweepback, nil. Empty weight, 5,180 lb.; gross weight, 8,115 lb. Max. speed, 222 m.p.h.; cruising speed, 174 m.p.h.; initial rate of climb, 1,240 ft./min.; service ceiling, 25,500 ft.; take-off distance to 50 ft., 2,050 ft.; landing distance from 50 ft., 1,560 ft.; range, 800–1,200 miles (eight or six occupants respectively) at 15,000 ft.

1

2

1. *A Piaggio P.136L of the Italian Air Force.*
2. *and 3. The Piaggio P.166 in camouflage finish.*

3

PIAGGIO P.149 (Italy)

ADOPTED IN 1955 as the standard basic trainer for the Luftwaffe, the Piaggio P.149-D was developed from the P.148 primary trainer. The latter first flew on February 12, 1951, culminating a rapid development programme which occupied less than a year. The P.148 seated two side-by-side with an occasional third seat behind, and was powered by a 190 h.p. Lycoming O-435-A engine. One hundred were ordered for service with the Italian Air Force; a number of these were transferred to the Somali Air Corps in 1964.

The P.149 was derived from the P.148 as a four-seat tourer, with a retractable under-carriage and a 270 h.p. Lycoming GO-480 engine. A prototype first flew on June 19, 1953. A version equipped to the requirements of the Luftwaffe was designated P.149-D and was produced in Germany by Focke-Wulf. Piaggio supplied 72, followed by 190 by Focke-Wulf, the first of these being delivered in November 1957.

The P.149-D is used by the Luftwaffe in the basic training rôle as a two-seater and for communications with five seats.

Span, 36 ft. 6 in.; length, 28 ft. 9½ in.; height, 9 ft. 6 in.; wing area, 203 sq. ft.; aspect ratio, 6.6; sweepback, nil.
Empty weight, 2,557 lb.; gross weight, 3,704 lb.
Max. speed, 192 m.p.h. at sea level; cruising speed, 165 m.p.h.; initial rate of climb, 980 ft./min.; service ceiling, 19,800 ft.; take-off distance to 50 ft., 1,328 ft.; landing distance from 50 ft., 1,033 ft.; range, 680 miles.

---

1. *A prototype Piaggio P.149 in Italian Air Force markings.*
2. *A Piaggio P.149 D for the Luftwaffe.*
3. *A Swiss Air Force Pilatus P.3.*

PILATUS P.3 (Switzerland)

THE PILATUS company designed the P.3 to meet particular requirements of the Swiss Air Force for a trainer covering the full syllabus of pilot training from *ab initio* to intermediate stage. The design is orthodox with tandem seating, all-metal construction and a 260 h.p. Lycoming GO-435-C2A engine.

A private venture prototype of the P.3 (HB-HON) was flown on September 3, 1953 and a pre-production batch of 18 was ordered by the Swiss Air Force. Extensive evaluation of these pre-production aircraft led to a further order for 50 P.3s to replace the North American T-6s in service in Switzerland. The first production aircraft flew on May 8, 1956, and six were also later supplied to the Brazilian Navy.

The P.3 is used for armament training as well as other phases of the training programme, and carries a 7.9 mm. gun pod, 5 cm. Oerlikon rockets, or 26.5 lb. bombs beneath the wings.
Span, 34 ft. 1 in.; length, 28 ft. 8½ in.; height, 10 ft. 0 in.; wing area, 178 sq. ft.; aspect ratio, 6.55; sweepback, nil.
Empty weight, 2,310 lb.; gross weight, 3,300 lb.
Max. speed, 192 m.p.h. at sea level; cruising speed, 155 m.p.h.; initial rate of climb, 1,378 ft./min.; service ceiling, 18,040 ft.; take-off distance to 50 ft., 1,110 ft.; landing distance from 50 ft., 1,245 ft.; range, 466 miles.

PILATUS PC-6 PORTER (Switzerland)

SINCE ITS FIRST FLIGHT in 1959, the Pilatus Porter has attracted considerable attention for its STOL capabilities which allow it to compete, under many circumstances, with the performance of a helicopter. Most of the fifty or so Porters built by 1964 have gone into commercial operation but military interest in the type is growing. The Colombian Air Force has purchased six Porters and Turbo Porters, one example of the latter serves with the Israeli Air Force, and the Swiss Army was planning to place an order in 1964.

The Porter was designed in 1957 to provide a general utility aircraft with good flying characteristics and the ability to operate from small, unprepared fields. The cabin was large enough for up to ten occupants including the pilot, and provision was made for rapid conversion of the interior for various rôles. These can include freight-carrying, aerial photography, supply dropping, parachute training, agricultural dusting and spraying and casualty evacuation (with two stretchers and five seats).

Skis, floats and combination wheel-ski gear can be fitted to the Porter, and oversize low-pressure tyres are used for operations from soft ground.

Five prototypes of the Porter were built and the first of these (HB-FAN) flew for the first time on May 4, 1959. These aircraft were powered by 340 h.p. Lycoming GSO-480-B1A6 engines, which became the standard power-plant in the PC-6/340 for which type approval was obtained on November 9, 1961. With high-pressure tyres and increased gross weight, the designation becomes PC-6/340-H1, while the -H2 has a still further increase in gross weight.

The 350 h.p. Lycoming IGO-540-A1A is available as an alternative powerplant, in the PC-6/350 variants.

Considerably improved performance resulted

from installation of the Turboméca Astazou turboprop in a Porter (HB-FAD, first flown May 2, 1961) and a number of PC-6A Turbo Porters had been sold by 1964. Two were extensively demonstrated by the U.S. agents, Fairchild-Hiller Corp. and three have been purchased for anti-guerilla operations in South East Asia. Five of the six Porters ordered by the Colombian Air Force are also Astazou powered.

Another variant of the Turbo Porter, the PC-6B, is powered by a Pratt & Whitney PT6A-6 engine and this (HB-FBM) first flew on May 1, 1964.

Data for the Astazou engined Turbo Porter:
Span, 49 ft. 10½ in.; length, 36 ft. 1 in.; height, 10 ft. 6 in.; wing area, 307 sq. ft.; aspect ratio, 8; sweepback, nil.
Empty equipped weight, 2,248 lb.; gross weight, 4,850 lb.
Max. speed (in a dive), 174 m.p.h.; cruising speed, 155 m.p.h.; initial rate of climb, 1,700 ft./min.; service ceiling, 28,000 ft.; take-off distance to 50 ft., 672 ft.; landing distance from 50 ft., 544 ft.; max. range, 620 miles.

1. *A civil-registered PC-6/360 Porter.*
2. *A Turbo-Porter being demonstrated for the U.S. Army.*
3. *Israeli Air Force Turbo-Porter.*

POTEZ **MAGISTER** (France)

Potez C.M.170s of the French Air Force in formation.

ONE OF THE MOST successful basic jet trainers produced to date, the Magister was developed originally by the Fouga company under the direction of M. Pierre Mauboussin, to take advantage of the series of small gas turbines produced by the Turboméca company. The French Air Force placed a contract for three prototypes of the C.M.170 design in June 1951, the aircraft being designed to meet official requirements for a basic jet trainer.

The first C.M.170 flew on July 23, 1952 and a year later a pre-production batch of ten was ordered, the first of these flying on July 7, 1954. Initial production orders had already been placed, in January of that year, and by 1964 some 400 examples had been produced in the following variants:

C.M.170-1. Basic production trainer for French Air Force, powered by 880 lb.s.t. Marboré IIA turbojets. First order for 95 placed on January 13, 1954 and first production aircraft flown on February 29, 1956. During 1954, the Potez company joined with Etablissements Fouga to form Potez-Air Fouga, which company was responsible for Magister development until September 1961, when it was completely absorbed by Potez. In addition to French Air Force orders, this version was exported to Belgium (45), Austria (18), Germany (40), Cambodia (4), Finland (18) and Morocco.

Licences to build the Magister have been obtained by Finland, Austria, Israel and Germany. In Finland, the Magister is being produced by Valmet OY, which has an Air Force order for 52. In Israel, production of 20 is being handled by Israel Aircraft Industries. Production of 210 Magisters in Germany was handled by the Flugzeug Union Sud, an amalgamation of the Heinkel and Messerschmitt companies.

C.M.170-2. A 1964 contract from the French Air Force for 130 Magisters specified the use of 1,058 lb. Marboré VI turbojets, leading to this change of designation.

C.M.173. Known as the Super Magister, this version has many improvements in addition to the use of 1,058 lb. Marboré VI turbojets. The nose has been lengthened and the cockpits

enlarged to accommodate ejection seats. Integral tanks replace the original flexible bag tanks in the wings, giving increased capacity. Size of ailerons has been increased and power boost added. The prototype first flew on June 10, 1964, and was subsequently re-designated Potez P.94A as the prototype of a proposed counter-insurgency and light ground attack aircraft, P.94B.

C.M.175 Zephyr. This version of the Magister was developed for the French Navy with modifications for shipboard use. These comprise, primarily, the addition of an arrester hook, strengthening of the undercarriage, and sliding instead of upwards-opening cockpit canopies. Two prototypes (the first flown on July 31, 1956) were followed by 45 production Zephyrs, the first of which flew on May 30, 1959.

C.M.191. This development of the Magister design has a new wider front fuselage with four seats. It retains dual controls, and is intended for the liaison and communications rôle in military or civil guise. The C.M.191 was conceived as a joint Franco-German venture and a prototype, financed by the West German Government, was built by Heinkel. The first flight was made on March 19, 1962.

Data for the C.M.170-1 follow:
Span, 37 ft. 5 in.; length, 33 ft. 0 in.; height, 9 ft. 2 in.; wing area, 186.1 sq. ft.; aspect ratio, 7.42; sweepback, nil.
Empty equipped weight, 4,740 lb.; max. gross weight, 7,055 lb.
Max. speed, 444 m.p.h. at 30,000 ft. (Mach.= 0.82); initial rate of climb, 2,950 ft./min.; service ceiling, 36,000 ft.; take-off distance to 50 ft., 3,050 ft.; range, 735 miles at 30,000 ft.; endurance, 2 hr. 40 min. at 30,000 ft.

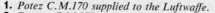
1. *Potez C.M.170 supplied to the Luftwaffe.*
2. *Potez C.M.170 in Austrian Air Force markings.*
3. *An Israeli-built Magister.*
4. *The Potez-Heinkel C.M.191 prototype.*

1

2

3

4

SAAB **105** (Sweden)

The prototype Saab 105 in flight.

SWEDEN'S PRINCIPAL AIRCRAFT manufacturer, Svenska Aeroplan Aktiebolaget (Saab) began development of a general purpose twin-jet aircraft in 1959. The project was a private venture by the company, which anticipated an eventual requirement for an intermediate trainer for the Royal Swedish Air Force as well as an overseas market for such a type in both military and civil guise.

Soon after preliminary studies had been started by Saab, the R.Sw.A.F. (Flygvapnet) made known its official requirements for a new training aircraft, and from the Spring of 1960 onwards, the design of the Saab 105 took full account of this outline specification, although it remained wholly a private venture.

During 1961, the Flygvapnet requirement was modified to add light attack capability to the proposed new trainer, so that the aircraft could also be used for direct support of Army forces in North Sweden and of Naval forces off the Swedish coast. This new requirement was also accommodated in the design from the outset.

After a preliminary evaluation of a number of foreign jet trainers during 1961, the Flygvapnet informed Saab that it was prepared in principle to purchase the Saab 105 in substantial quantities provided it was able to comply with the specification. Prototypes built at Saab risk would be evaluated before an order was confirmed.

With a major market thus virtually assured, Saab proceeded to build two prototypes, first flown respectively on June 29, 1963 and June 17, 1964. The first prototype was handed over for Air Force testing on November 20, 1963 and on March 6, 1964 the Swedish Government authorized the Flygvapnet to proceed with a contract for 130 aircraft. Deliveries were scheduled to begin in November 1965.

The training version of the Saab 105 is designated Sk60 by the Air Force, while the attack version will be designated A60. An order for 20 A60s was projected in the 1964–65 budget but all Sk60s will have six wing pick-up points for bombs, rockets, guided missiles or cannon pods. The Saab 105 can be equipped as a staff or executive transport with four seats, but in the training and attack rôle has side-by-side seating for the crew of two, with ejection seats.

No fixed armament is carried by the Saab 105, but a variety of different weapons can be carried on the wing pick-ups. These include twelve 13.5 cm. rocket projectiles; six 265 lb. or two 550 lb. bombs; two 30 mm. cannon or two guided misiles.

Development of the Turboméca Aubisque turbofan engines which power the Saab 105 is expected to increase the power from 1,540 lb. to 1,650 lb. static thrust in the production aircraft. The prototype was the first aircraft in which the Aubisque had flown.

Span, 31 ft. 2 in.; length, 34 ft. 5 in.; height, 8 ft. 10 in.; wing area, 175 sq. ft.
Empty weight, 5,534 lb.; max. gross weight (trainer), 7,605 lb.; max. gross weight (attack), 8,760 lb.
Max. speed, 475 m.p.h. at 20,000 ft.; max. cruising speed, 438 m.p.h. at 30,000 ft.; initial rate of climb, 3,940 ft./min.; service ceiling, 44,300 ft.; take-off distance to 50 ft., 2,530 ft.; landing distance from 50 ft., 2,890 ft.; range, 1,120 miles at 30,000 ft. in training configuration; endurance, 3.8 hours at 30,000 ft.

1. *An in-flight view of the prototype Saab 105.*
2. *The Saab 105 carrying 12 rockets.*
3. *Air-to-air missiles under the Saab 105's wing.*
4. *The Saab 105 prototype with wing fences removed and extended air intakes and exhaust fairings.*

SAAB **91** SAFIR (Sweden)

A Saab 91D in Austrian Air Force markings.

SINCE THE SAAB Safir went into production in Sweden shortly after the end of the War, a total of 241 has been sold to six air forces, in addition to 82 sold for civil use. Production was continuing in 1964.

The Safir was originally projected as a two-seat tourer and trainer, but before the designs were completed, a third seat was added in the rear of the cockpit. The general lines of the aircraft appear to have been influenced by the design of the Bücker Bü 181 Bestmann, which served with the Royal Swedish Air Force, but in structural design Saab drew on their own wide experience of military aircraft types.

The prototype Safir, SE-APN, was first flown on November 20, 1945 and was designated Saab 91. It was powered by a 130 h.p. de Havilland Gipsy Major 1C engine, but the 145 h.p. Gipsy Major 10 was earmarked for the production model Saab 91A. The prototype was subsequently flown on floats to obtain clearance for the Safir seaplane.

Saab 91A. Initial three-seat production version with Gipsy Major 10 engine. Full dual control for pilot and passenger side-by-side, with a second passenger on the starboard side and a luggage compartment behind the pilot. In place of the two passengers, a stretcher can be carried alongside the pilot. Production of the Saab 91A totalled 49, of which ten were supplied to the Royal Swedish Air Force with the designation Tp91 for communications centres and 16 went to the Imperial Ethiopian Air Force as trainers. The remainder were sold for civil use.

Saab 91B. On January 15, 1949, the first flight was made of a new version of the Safir, in which the Gipsy Major engine was replaced by a 190 h.p. Lycoming O-435-A flat-six unit. This gave a considerable improvement in overall performance. In June 1951, the Royal Swedish Air Force adopted the Saab 91B as its standard primary trainer to replace the Bücker Bestmann and ordered 75 examples. As the Saab company was at this time fully occupied with J29 and J21R production, arrangements were made for the Safir to be built under licence in Holland by De Schelde at Dordrecht.

The R.Sw.A.F. designation for this version was Sk50B in the trainer category. The Imperial Ethiopian Air Force also purchased 17 of this version while the Royal Norwegian Air Force acquired 25 of a similar variant designated

[Continued on p. 108

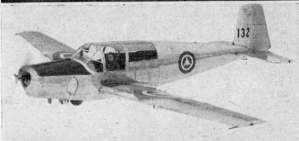

1. A Swedish Air Force Sk.50B, the Saab 91C.
2. Ethiopian Air Force Saab 91C.
3. Norwegian Saab 91B.
4. Tunisian Saab 91B.
5. The first Saab 91D for the Finnish Air Force.

5

SCOTTISH AVIATION TWIN PIONEER (Great Britain)

DESIGN OF THE TWIN-ENGINED general purpose Twin Pioneer began in 1951 following the successful introduction of the single-engined Pioneer. In 1956, the Royal Air Force decided to purchase a quantity of Twin Pioneers for use overseas, particularly in support of land forces engaged in local "brush-fire" wars.

Total production for the R.A.F. included 32 aircraft designated CC.Mk.1 and four CC.Mk.2s with structural changes, powered by 540 h.p. Alvis Leonides 128 piston radial engines. All were subsequently brought up to the civil Twin Pioneer Series 3 standard by uprating of the engine to 615 h.p. Leonides 138s. These aircraft, the first of which flew on August 29, 1957, were allocated primarily to squadrons serving in Aden, East Africa and Singapore.

Accommodation in the military Twin Pioneer is for 12 equipped troops or six stretchers plus five sitting casualties. Light-weight racks can be fitted under the stub wings between the fuselage and mainwheels, with a capacity of 1,000 lb. each side.

Four Twin Pioneers were ordered by the Royal Malayan Air Force in 1957 and another ten were purchased subsequently.

Span, 76 ft. 6 in.; length, 45 ft. 3 in.; height, 12 ft. 1 in.; wing area, 670 sq. ft.; aspect ratio, 8.73; sweepback, nil.
Empty equipped weight, 10,200 lb.; gross weight, 14,600 lb.
Max. speed, 165 m.p.h. at 2,000 ft.; cruising speed, 140 m.p.h. at 7,000 ft.; initial rate of climb, 1,250 ft./min.; service ceiling, 20,000 ft.; take-off distance to 50 ft., 1,150 ft.; landing distance from 50 ft., 1,150 ft.; range with 3,800 lb. load, 210 miles; range with max. fuel, 733 miles.

1. *A production model Twin Pioneer in R.A.F. service.*
2. *A Twin Pioneer with door removed for supply-dropping trials.*
3. *A Twin Pioneer of the Royal Malaysian Air Force in company with a single-engined Pioneer.*

SAAB 91 SAFIR (Sweden)
[Continued from p. 107]

Saab 91B-2. Another 17 of the "B" models were built for civil use.

Saab 91C. First flown in September 1953, this variant introduced provision for a fourth seat behind the pilot. The gross weight was increased at the expense of a small reduction in performance since the powerplant remained the same as in the Saab 91B. Saab resumed production of the Safir at the beginning of 1955 and stepped up the rate of production in 1959 when the Royal Swedish Air Force ordered 14 "C" model Safirs as Sk50Cs. The Imperial Ethiopian Air Force also purchased 10, and another 11 were built for the civil market.

Saab 91D. Final production version of the Safir, the "D" reverts to a lower powered engine, the 180 h.p. Lycoming O-360-A1A. This is made possible, with little loss in performance, by use of a constant speed propeller and a reduction in empty weight. Other new features are a more powerful generator to match the extensive electric and radio equipment; and Goodyear single-disc brakes.

In July 1958, the first military order for the Saab 91D came from the Finnish Air Force and this order was eventually increased to 35. The Tunisian Air Force ordered 15 and delivery of 24 to the Austrian Air Force began in 1964 —12 for pilot training and 12 for navigation training. Production of this version totalled 105.

Data for the Saab 91D:
Span, 34 ft. 9 in.; length, 26 ft. 4 in.; height, 7 ft. 2½ in.; wing area, 146 sq. ft.; aspect ratio, 8.3; sweepback, nil.
Empty weight, 1,570 lb.; gross weight (aerobatic), 2,315 lb.; gross weight (normal category), 2,660 lb.
Max. speed, 165 m.p.h. at sea level; cruising speed, 137 m.p.h. at sea level, 66 per cent power; initial rate of climb, 800 ft./min.; service ceiling, 16,400 ft.; take-off distance to 50 ft., 2,030 ft.; landing distance from 50 ft., 1,800 ft.; range, 660 miles at 5,000 ft.

S.E.E.M.S. **MS760 PARIS** (France)

THE PARIS WAS THE FIRST and only jet aircraft design of the well-known French aircraft manufacturer Morane-Saulnier. First flown in 1954, it was still the subject of development in 1963 when the company ran into financial difficulties and was acquired by the Potez group. The new title of Societe d'Exploitation des Etablissements Morane-Saulnier (S.E.E.M.S.) was then adopted and work on the Paris III is being continued by this company.

The MS760 was conceived as a high-speed communications and luxury touring aircraft and was one of the first applications of jet power to a small passenger-carrying aeroplane suitable for civilian as well as military use.

The four-seat Paris can carry a variety of armament if operating in the light ground attack rôle or as an armament trainer. Two 7.5 mm. machine guns can be mounted in the fuselage nose with a cine gun and a gyro gun sight in the cockpit. Underwing provision can be made for up to 12 rockets or eight 112 lb. bombs or two 260 lb. and two 112 lb. bombs.

Three versions of the Paris have appeared, as follows:

MS760A Paris I. Prototype first flew on July 29, 1954 and first production model on February 27, 1958. Powered by two 880 lb.s.t. Turboméca Marboré II turbojets. Purchased in small numbers by the French Air Force and French Navy for use in the communications rôle. Other sales included 36 for Argentina and 29 for Brazil. The aircraft for Argentina were delivered unassembled and were put together in the State factory at Cordoba (first flight, October 27, 1958), going into service with the Argentine Air Force. The 29 aircraft for Brazil included ten for liaison, twelve trainers and seven equipped for photo-survey duties.

MS760B Paris II. Similar to Paris I but powered by 1,058 lb.s.t. Marboré VI turbojets. Detail changes included introducing integral fuel tanks in the wing leading edge, to increase the fuel capacity by 97 Imp. gallons, adding electric anti-icing of the air intakes and increasing cabin pressure differential and air conditioning. Deliveries of the Paris II included one for Brazil, where the type was put into production to meet a Government order for 48.

MS760C Paris III. One prototype has been built of this six-seat development of the Paris II, with similar powerplant. The first flight was made on February 28, 1964. Intended primarily for the commercial and executive market, the Paris III will dispense with wing-tip tanks on the production version, and have a longer wing span with extra internal fuel.

Span, 33 ft. 3 in.; length, 33 ft. 7 in.; height, 8 ft. 6 in.; wing area, 194 sq. ft.; aspect ratio, 5.12.

Empty equipped weight, 4,557 lb.; gross weight, 8,380 lb.; max. landing weight, 6,945 lb.

Max. speed, 432 m.p.h. at 25,000 ft.; max. cruising speed, 393 m.p.h. at 16,400 ft.; initial rate of climb, 2,460 ft./min.; service ceiling, 39,370 lb.; take-off distance to 50 ft., 5,415 ft.; range, 1,080 miles at 25,000 ft.

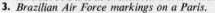

1. *The prototype Paris, F-BGVO.*
2. *An MS760 Paris in French Air Force colours.*
3. *Brazilian Air Force markings on a Paris.*

SHORT BELFAST C.Mk.1 (Great Britain)

The first Short Belfast in flight.

A PRODUCTION CONTRACT for ten strategic freighters of new design was placed with Short Bros. and Harland by R.A.F. Transport Command in 1960. Known originally as the Britannic and subsequently re-named the Belfast, the new type was the first military freighter ever ordered in Britain specifically for strategic duties. Its cargo hold cross-section is greater than that of any other military freighter built to date, with a clear 12 ft. width and height available over the whole length.

Design work which led eventually to the Belfast began as a private venture by Short Bros. following the PD.16 project for a smaller tactical transport. No official specification or Operational Requirement for a strategic freighter had been drawn up, but Short Bros. were not alone in seeing the need for such a type and the prospective order became the subject of intense competition.

The earliest Short studies were for a completely new aircraft, similar in overall configuration to the Douglas C-133 and powered by four Bristol Orion engines. The need to minimize initial costs in order to gain official support led to these proposals being dropped in favour of a design based on the wing and tail unit of the Bristol Britannia—already built under licence by Short Bros. Rolls-Royce Tyne engines, at their R.Ty.12 rating, were selected in place of the Bristol Siddeley Proteus, however. From the outset, possible civil orders were foreseen and when the Belfast was ordered, the R.A.F. directed that it should be developed to the standards of a full Public Transport Category certificate of airworthiness.

The 12 ft. square section of the Belfast's fuselage was dictated primarily by the size of Army vehicles and other military stores which might need to be carried. These dimensions were provided within a fuselage of circular cross-section with a maximum width of 16 ft. 1 in. and a length of 84 ft. 4 in. including the rear loading ramp. A second, upper deck can be fitted at the front of the cabin to provide maximum seating capacity of 201 troops.

Interesting features of the Belfast, in addition to its large size and rear loading ramp (the first of its kind, incorporated in a minimum drag afterbody, adopted in a British aircraft), include the semi-podded nacelles for the Tyne engines, provision for flight refuelling and autoland capability using Smith's Automatic Flight Control System Mk.29. The engines specified initially are 5,505 e.h.p. Tyne Mk. 101s; a water-injection version of this engine, the Mk. 101W, is also available at a rating of 5,730 e.h.p.

The first Belfast (XR362) flew for the first time at Belfast on January 5, 1964 and the second flew on May 1. These two aircraft were allocated to complete the flight test programme in 850 hours in 18 months. Full autoland equipment was first installed in the third Belfast (XR364) which flew on August 19, 1964. Deliveries to the R.A.F. were scheduled for the autumn of 1965.

Several other variants of the Belfast have been projected since the initial S.C.5/10 version was ordered. None of these had been ordered up to the end of 1964.

Data for the Belfast C.Mk.1:
Span, 158 ft. 9½ in.; length, 135 ft. 5 in.; height, 47 ft. 0 in.; wing area, 2,455 sq. ft.; aspect ratio, 10.22; sweepback, 7.05 degrees.
Empty equipped weight, 125,000 lb.; gross weight, 225,000 lb.; payload, 80,000 lb.; landing weight, 215,000 lb.
Max. cruising speed, 358 m.p.h.; take-off distance required, 7,300 ft.; landing distance required, 5,200 ft.; range, 970 miles with 80,000 lb. payload at 340 m.p.h.; range, 5,200 miles with 19,300 lb. payload at 340 m.p.h.

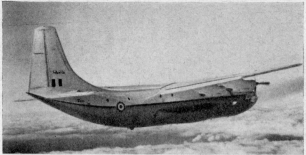

1

2

3

4

1. *Belfast XR362 in flight.*
2. *The first take-off of Belfast XR362.*
3. *A Belfast with wheels and flaps down.*
4. *Belfast XR362 taxi-ing.*

SOKO GALEB (Jugoslavia)

WITH WORKS AT MOSTAR, the Preduzece Soko concern is part of the State-controlled aircraft industry which was established in Jugoslavia following the end of the War in 1945. Its activities have included the licence-production of the Westland S-55 helicopter and—since 1958—development of the Galeb (Gull) jet trainer.

In configuration, the Galeb is similar to such contemporaries as the Macchi MB326 (p. 84), the Hunting Jet Provost (p. 71) and the Fuji T1A (p. 48)—and like all these three, it is powered by a Bristol Siddeley Viper turbojet. For use in the prototype programme, three Viper ASV.11s were purchased and the first of these, delivered in the autumn of 1959,

1. *A production model of the Galeb.*
2. *The Galeb in Yugoslav Air Force colours.*
3. *Second prototype Galeb with smaller ventral fin.*

powered the prototype Galeb on its first flight in May 1961. A second prototype followed in 1962, with modifications.

Production of the Galeb was reported to have begun at Mostar during 1963 and a substantial number of Vipers was ordered from Bristol Siddeley in the same year. Deliveries were expected to begin towards the end of 1964, for the Galeb to become the standard jet trainer in use with the Jugoslav Air Force.

The design aim for the Galeb was to produce an aircraft which could safely be used for *ab initio* training by pupils with no prior flying experience, but at the same time having adequate performance for more advanced training including navigation and armament training.

The Galeb has tandem seating for pupil and instructor, with complete duplication of controls and equipment. Both cockpits have a Folland lightweight ejection seat.

Construction of the wing is two spar with stressed skin covering. The wing is made up of a centre section integral with the fuselage, and two mainplanes. Ailerons are aerodynamically balanced and manually controlled, in common with the elevators and rudder. Hydraulically operated flaps are fitted. Fuel tanks at the wing-tips are jettisonable and supplement the internal fuel capacity.

Standard armament comprises two 12.7 mm. Colt-Browning guns in the nose; bombs or rockets can be carried beneath the wings when required.

The Viper Mk. 22-6 supplied for production models of the Galeb is rated at 2,500 lb. thrust for take-off.

Span, 34 ft. 0½ in. (38 ft. 2 in. over tip tanks); length, 33 ft. 11 in.; height, 10 ft. 10 in.; wing area, 209.14 sq. ft.; aspect ratio, 5.55; sweepback, nil.

Empty equipped weight, 5,485 lb.; gross weight (internal fuel), 7,438 lb.; gross weight (with tip tanks), 8,200 lb.

Max. speed, 505 m.p.h. at 2,350 ft.; initial rate of climb, 4,500 ft./min.; take-off distance to 50 ft., 2,100 ft.; landing distance from 50 ft., 2,340 ft.; max. range (with tip tanks), 770 miles at 9,842 ft.; max. endurance, 2 hours 30 minutes.

TS-11 ISKRA (Poland)

LIKE MANY OTHER major air forces, the Polish Air Force decided towards the end of the 'fifties that basic pilot training should in future be given on a jet-powered aeroplane. At the time this conclusion was reached, the piston-engined TS-8 Bies was in service at Polish military training schools, and a specification was drawn up for a jet trainer to replace it.

Similar aircraft were under development concurrently in Czechoslovakia (L 29 Delfin—p. 98) and the U.S.S.R. (Yak-30—pp. 118–119) and there is some evidence to suggest that all three were built to a common requirement which embraced the needs of the Soviet Air Force and the Eastern European bloc of Soviet satellite countries. The three types were all evaluated in the U.S.S.R., leading to choice of the L 29 with the Polish design rated in second place.

Wing root intakes are featured, resembling in shape and location those of the Macchi MB326 and incorporating boundary layer fences at the fuselage sides. Also in common with the MB326 and several other basic jet trainers, the TS-11 features tandem seating for its pupil and instructor. Lightweight ejection seats are installed in the cockpit, which is covered by a one-piece rearward-hinged jettisonable canopy.

The TS-11 appears to have a comparatively thin wing section for reasonable high-speed performance, but the wing is not swept back. This configuration combines satisfactory handling qualities with an opportunity to demonstrate high sub-sonic phenomena including buffet. Hydraulic power is used for aileron operation, the elevators and rudder being manual.

Power is provided by a single axial flow turbojet of Polish origin, rated at approximately 1,900 lb. static thrust and designated TO-2.

Development of the TS-11 was initiated in the design office attached to the Osrodek Konstrukcji Lotniczych (Aircraft Construction Centre) at Warsaw-Okecie. There, the prototype made its first flight on February 5, 1960. Production is centred at another state factory, the Wytwornia Sprzetu Komunikacyjnego at Mielec, and the first production Iskra was handed over to the Polish Air Force in March 1963.

In common with other jet trainers in the same category, the TS-11 has considerable potential in the ground-attack rôle. Armament can include forward firing guns in the nose and a typical selection of underwing stores including bombs, rockets or fuel tanks.

Span, 32 ft. 10 in.; length, 36 ft. 1 in.; height, 10 ft. 10 in.; wing area, 381 sq. ft.
Gross weight, 7,495 lb.
Max. speed, 497 m.p.h. at 20,000 ft.; service ceiling, 39,370 ft.; take-off run, 1,650–2,600 ft.; landing run, 1,950–2,250 ft.

1. *A production model Iskra in Polish Air Force service.*
2. *The Iskra in flight.*
3. *A prototype Iskra showing the upwards-hinged canopy.*

TRANSALL **C.160** (France/Germany)

The first Transall C.160 in slow flight with wheels and flaps down.

ONE OF THE FIRST examples of multi-nation design, development and production of a new aircraft, the Transall C.160 is the outcome of a programme started during 1958. At that time, the German aircraft industry had established several links with French aircraft manufacturers through the production of French aircraft under licence. One such programme was the production of the Nord Noratlas (p. 90) in Germany and when this machine's successor was projected, the existing Franco-German link was seen as the basis for further collaboration.

The specification called for an aircraft with the ability to fly an 8,000 kg. (17,637 lb.) payload for 4,500 km. (2,800 miles). It was to be capable of operating from unprepared, 2,000 ft. landing strips and the choice of engines was to be between two Rolls-Royce Tynes, two Bristol Orion or four Rolls-Royce Darts. In December 1958 submissions by Nord and Weser were selected for further study and on January 28, 1959 the two Governments formally agreed to go ahead with the project sharing development costs equally. The Transport Alliance (name "Transall") was set up to co-ordinate the project.

An order for five prototypes followed in March 1960—three for flight test, one for static testing and one for fatigue testing. Nord became responsible for the French share of the C.160 with Weser and Hamburger sharing in the German portion.

Design of the C.160 follows "classic" lines for a military transport. The fuselage provides a constant cross-section in the cabin of 9 ft. 7 in. by 10 ft. 2½ in. for a length of 42 ft. Loading of vehicles and heavy freight is through a rear entrance with clam-shell type doors and a loading ramp; in addition, there are paratroop doors on each side of the rear fuselage and a cargo door forward in the port side. The fuselage can accommodate up to 81 troops or paratroops; 62 stretchers with attendants; or a wide range of military vehicles.

The Rolls-Royce Tyne, in its 5,665 s.h.p. R.Ty.20 version, was selected to power the C.160. While engines for the prototypes were supplied by Rolls-Royce, production aircraft will have Tynes built by Hispano-Suiza in France.

During 1962, France and Germany agreed to sponsor construction of six pre-production C.160s and plans were made for the production of an initial batch of 200 aircraft. Of this quantity, 50 were to be earmarked for l'Armée de l'Air and the other 150 for the Luftwaffe; the latter subsequently reduced its requirement to 110.

The first of the three C.160 prototypes, allocated the German serial number D-9507, was assembled by Nord and was first flown on February 25, 1963. It was followed by the second, assembled by Weser, on May 25, 1963 and by the third, put together by H.F.B. at Hamburg, on February 19, 1964. Delivery of production C.160s was scheduled to begin at the end of 1965.

Span, 131 ft. 3 in.; length, 103 ft. 6 in.; height, 38 ft. 2½ in.; wing area, 1,722.1 sq. ft.; aspect ratio, 10; sweepback, nil.
Empty equipped weight, 58,500 lb.; max. payload, 33,000 lb.; gross weight, 102,600 lb.; max. landing weight, 100,700 lb.
Cruising speed, 317 m.p.h. at 24,250 ft.; initial rate of climb, 1,885 ft./min.; service ceiling, 27,700 ft.; take-off distance to 35 ft., 2,000 ft.; landing distance from 50 ft., 1,900 ft.; range with max. payload, 1,175 miles; range with 17,600 lb. payload, 2,400 miles.

1

2

3

4

1. *The first Transalls in flight.*
2. *Transall D-9507 in company with a Nord 262.*
3. *The third Transall, D-9509.*
4. *First prototype Transall, D-9507.*

VC10 C.Mk.1 (Great Britain)

SCHEDULED FOR DELIVERY to R.A.F. Transport Command in 1966, the VC10 is the largest aeroplane (in terms of gross weight) ever ordered for military service in Britain. A derivative of the civil VC10 which entered service with B.O.A.C. in April 1964, the R.A.F. version has a number of special features for its military rôle.

Dimensionally, the VC10 C.Mk.1 is the same as the "Standard" VC10 version, of which B.O.A.C. has 12 and which is also used by British United and Ghana Airways. It is powered, however, by four 22,500 lb. static thrust Conway R. Co.43 Mk. 550 turbofans of the type used in the commercial Super VC10. The extra power of these engines makes it possible for the Transport Command version to operate at higher weights—up to 322,000 lb.

1. *An impression of the R.A.F. VC10 with flight-refuelling probe.*
2. *The prototype VC10, G-ARTA.*
3. *A B.U.A. VC10 showing freight-loading door.*

gross. This higher weight, and the special requirements of the military rôle, have led to some minor structural alterations. Also like the Super VC10, the R.A.F. version has an integral fuel tank in the fin.

Like the version of the VC10 used by B.U.A., the C.Mk.1 has a large freight-loading door in the forward fuselage port side. The entire fuselage floor is specially reinforced to cater for heavy military loads. A flight refuelling probe is carried in the nose of the VC10 to permit refuelling in flight from Victor tankers.

For trooping duties, the R.A.F.'s VC10 can carry 150 troops, compared with 135 passengers in the airline version, and these will normally be in rearward-facing seats. The normal airline-type luggage racks will be retained in the cabin, plus the standard "hard trim" wall panels in plastic.

Development of the VC10 began late in 1956 primarily to meet a B.O.A.C. requirement for an aeroplane that would operate with economic payloads out of restricted airfields. A contract for 35 VC10s was signed by B.O.A.C. in 1958, and the first example (G-ARTA) made its first flight on June 29, 1963.

An initial R.A.F. order, for five aircraft, was announced in 1961 and a further six were ordered in 1962. When, in the summer of 1964, B.O.A.C. reduced its requirement for a fleet of Super VC10s, the R.A.F. was able to acquire three of these aircraft also, to make a total of 14. Although the three last-mentioned aircraft had been started as Super VC10s it is expected that all 14 for the R.A.F. will in fact be of a common type, identified by the manufacturer's Type number of 1106.

Span, 146 ft. 2 in.; length, 158 ft. 8 in.; height, 39 ft. 6 in.; wing area, 2,932 sq. ft.; aspect ratio, 7.5; sweepback, 32 degrees 30 minutes.
Empty equipped weight, 147,028 lb.; payload, 57,400 lb.; gross weight, 322,000 lb.; max. landing weight, 225,000 lb.
Cruising speed, 564 m.p.h.; initial rate of climb, 1,920 ft./min.; service ceiling, 42,000 ft.; take-off distance to 50 ft., 8,100 ft.; landing distance from 50 ft., 6,180 ft.; range, 3,950 miles with full payload at 564 m.p.h. at 30,000 ft.

VOUGHT-HILLER-RYAN XC-142A (U.S.A.)

ROLLED OUT ON June 17, 1964 in preparation for ground and flight trials in the second half of the year, the XC-142A is the first military support aircraft with VTOL capability. Its eventual production depends upon the success of initial evaluation with five prototypes, but its designation in the U.S. Defence Department's "C for cargo" category distinguishes it from other experimental VTOL types such as the Bell X-22 and Curtiss-Wright X-19.

The specification for a VTOL transport was issued to the U.S. industry in February 1961 and subsequent development was classified as the Support System SS478A for tri-service (Army, Navy, Air Force) use. The joint design submitted by Vought, Hiller and Ryan was selected in September 1961 and a go-ahead for construction of five examples was given in January 1962. Programme manager is the Vought Aeronautics Division of Ling-Temco-Vought Inc. with Hiller responsible for the transmission system and Ryan responsible for the rear fuselage and engine nacelles.

The XC-142A (company model number VHR447) is a tilt-wing type of convertiplane, in which the entire mainplane, complete with powerplant, can be tilted from horizontal through 100 degrees to beyond the vertical (to permit hovering in a tail wind). The four widely spaced engines—2,850 s.h.p. T64-GE-1 turboprops—drive 15.6 ft. diameter propellers; when the wing is vertical ailerons operate in the slipstream from these propellers to provide lateral control.

The fuselage of the XC-142A has been designed to carry a wide variety of payloads including, for example, 32 troops; 24 stretcher patients; a 2½-ton trailer; a 105 mm. howitzer and ¾-ton truck; palletizal freight, and so on. A tail-loading ramp is incorporated.

Following roll-out of the first XC-142A, it was assigned to a 50-hr. programme of ground running in a special cradle. The second aircraft was the first to fly, on September 29, 1964, and this aircraft was the first to complete a successful transition, from vertical to horizontal flight and back to vertical, on January 11, 1965. Delivery of the five aircraft to a tri-service evaluation team was scheduled from January 1965 to March 1966, with completion of the programme in July 1966.

Span, 67 ft. 6 in.; length, 58 ft. 1 in.; height, 26 ft. 1 in.; wing area, 534.5 sq. ft.; sweepback, nil.
Gross weight, 37,474 lb.
Max. speed, 374 knots at 20,000 ft.; cruising speed, 250 m.p.h. at sea level; initial climb, 6,800 ft./min.; operational ceiling, 25,000 ft.; ferry range, 3,800 miles.

1

2

3

1. *The first XC-142A, 62-5921, in test cradle.*
2. *The first XC-142A with engines vertical.*
3. *First take-off, second XC-142A, 62-5922.*

YAKOVLEV **YAK-18** (U.S.S.R.)

A single-seat Yak-18P with aft cockpit.

INTRODUCED IN 1946, the Yak-18 was designed to replace the ubiquitous UT-2, an earlier design by Aleksandir Yakovlev which served as the principal Soviet primary trainer throughout the period of the War. Final versions of the UT-2 incorporated several features which were retained in the Yak-18, including the "helmet" cowling for the engine and a long canopy over the two tandem cockpits.

Although re-designed structurally, the original Yak-18 differed little from the UT-2 in appearance apart from having a retractable main landing gear, the legs being attached close to the wing leading edge and folding backwards, with the wheels left to protrude partially from the wing. This arrangement afforded a measure of protection in the event of a forced landing, but was adopted as the simplest method of retracting the gear into the existing structure. Subsequently, a more extensive modification was designed to fold the legs inwards, as described below.

Initial production versions of the Yak-18 were powered by the 160 h.p. M-11FR radial engine with a typical Soviet "helmet" cowling which closely followed the lines of the five cylinders. Aircraft of this type were built in large quantities to equip the Soviet Air Force training schools and civil flying clubs, and for export. Countries known to have received Yak-18s include Afghanistan, Albania, Austria (no longer in service), Bulgaria, Peoples Republic of China, East Germany, Hungary, North Korea, Poland, Rumania and the United Arab Republic.

Successive development of the Yak-18 design has produced a number of major variants, as described below.

Yak-18U. To meet modern training needs, this variant has a nose-wheel undercarriage. The fuselage is lengthened by 18 in. to provide space for nose-wheel retraction and the main undercarriage legs are re-positioned on the rear wing spar to obtain the necessary wheelbase. The main legs retract forwards and the wheels are half-submerged in the wing, as in the Yak-18. Detailed re-design of the engine cowling and cockpit canopy was included. The Yak-18U, like the original Yak-18 was

given the NATO code-name of Max, and considerable numbers were exported to various of the nations listed above.

Yak-18A. A major re-design led to introduction of this version in 1957. The most important change was the introduction of a 260 h.p. Ivchenko AI-14R nine-cylinder radial engine with a fully circular cowling. The first series of Yak-18As had the same semi-retractable landing gear as the Yak-18U described above, but a later re-design allowed the main legs to fold inwards for the wheels to be totally enclosed. Both the Yak-18A and Yak-18P (below) have the NATO code-name of Mouse and have been exported to several East European countries.

Yak-18P. This single-seat advanced and aerobatic trainer exists in two distinct forms. The first and possibly most-used version had the front cockpit faired over, with a canopy over the rear cockpit and retained the semi-retractable undercarriage of the initial series of Yak-18As, with which it was in other respects identical. The other version, which has been used by Soviet competitors in a number of aerobatic contests, has the rear cockpit faired-in and is flown from the front cockpit; this version is based on the later series of Yak-18A with inwards, fully-retracting undercarriage.

Data for the latest version of the Yak-18A *follow:*

Span, 34 ft. 9¼ in.; length, 28 ft. 0 in.; height, 11 ft. 0 in.; wing area, 183 sq. ft.; aspect ratio, 6.3; sweepback, nil.
Empty weight, 2,260 lb.; gross weight, 2,900 lb.
Max. speed, 161 m.p.h.; cruising speed, 141 m.p.h.; initial rate of climb, 1,060 ft./min.; service ceiling, 16,600 ft.; range, 465 miles.

1

2

3

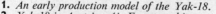

1. *An early production model of the Yak-18.*
2. *Yak-18 in Austrian Air Force markings.*
3. *A Yak-18A showing the smooth chord cowling.*
4. *A Yak-18P with forward cockpit.*

4

ADDENDA

DETAILS OF THE following aircraft became available too late for inclusion in the main body of the book.

DORNIER Do 31 (Germany)

PROTOTYPES OF THE Do 31 tactical V/STOL transport are under construction and are expected to fly in 1965. The design features a circular section fuselage, high wing and single tail unit. In the Do 31E prototypes, propulsion is by two Bristol Siddeley Pegasus 5 vectored-thrust engines in wing nacelles, with wing-tip pods each containing four Rolls-Royce RB.162 direct lift engines. Production versions, to be developed in collaboration with Hawker Siddeley, will have podded propulsion engines incorporating thrust deflection, and wing-mounted pods each containing five lift engines. The development programme includes the use of two hovering rigs, the first (flown in 1964) with four RB.108 engines and the second with the complete Do 31E powerplant. Data for the production version are: span, 64 ft. 0 in.; length, 70 ft. 6 in.; wing area, 602 sq. ft.; gross weight, 58,400 lb.; cruising speed, 465 m.p.h.; range, 1,120 miles.

FIAT G.222 (Italy)

AFTER A PERIOD of private venture development, the Fiat G.222 tactical V/STOL transport was given official support in the Spring of 1963 in the form of a research contract from the Italian Air Force. Development and construction of prototypes will eventually involve all major Italian aircraft manufacturers. The G.222 has a circular section fuselage with rear-loading doors, a high wing and a single tail unit. Powerplant comprises two Rolls-Royce Darts for forward propulsion with three Rolls-Royce R.B.162 lift jets in each nacelle. Span, 67 ft. 0 in.; length, 68 ft. 6 in.; gross weight, 39,460 lb.

HINDUSTAN HJT-16 (India)

FIRST FLOWN on September 4, 1964, the Hindustan HJT-16 is a basic jet trainer of wholly Indian design and construction. It is powered by a 2,500 lb. thrust Bristol Siddeley Viper ASV.11 turbojet and has side-by-side seating in a pressurized cockpit. An initial batch of 24 HJT-16s is being produced for the Indian Air Force. Gross weight is 6,490 lb.

PIAGGIO PD-808 (Italy)

DESIGNED BY Douglas Aircraft Co. and built in Italy by Piaggio, the PD-808 is a light jet utility aircraft intended for civil (executive) or military use. It provides accommodation for up to ten and is powered by two 3,000 lb. Bristol Siddeley Viper 525 turbojets, with the 2,850 lb.s.t. General Electric CF610-1 nominated as an alternative. The Italian Air Force ordered two prototypes for evaluation and the first of these flew on August 29, 1964. Span, 40 ft. 8½ in.; length, 41 ft. 7 in.; wing area, 225 sq. ft.; gross weight, 16,000 lb.; max. cruising speed, 555 m.p.h. at 32,000 ft.; range, 1,710 miles.

1

2

3

1. *Fiat G.222.*
2. *Hindustan HJT-16.*
3. *Piaggio PD-808.*
4. *Dornier Do 31E.*
5. *Dornier Do 31 production model.*

4

5